D1100446

A WHOLE NEW PLAN FOR LIVING

Achieving Balance and Wellness in a Changing World

Professor Jim Lucey is a Clinical Professor of Psychiatry at Trinity College Dublin (TCD) and a Consultant Psychiatrist at St Patrick's University Hospital in Dublin, Ireland.

Medical Director of St Patrick's Mental Health Service until his retirement in 2019, Jim Lucey has over thirty years' experience in clinical and academic psychiatry; previous clinical appointments include Consultant Psychiatrist at Connolly Hospital (HSE) Dublin, and Consultant Psychiatrist with responsibility for psychiatric intensive care at St Bartholomew's Hospital (NHS) London.

Formerly a governor of St Vincent's Psychiatric Hospital (HSE) in Dublin, and a member of the Health Committee of the Irish Medical Council, Professor Lucey was also a member of the board of the Mental Health Commission of Ireland.

He lives in Dublin.

Also by Jim Lucey

Understanding Psychiatric Treatment (with Gerald O'Mahony)
In My Room
The Life Well Lived

A WHOLE NEW PLAN FOR LIVING

Achieving Balance and Wellness in a Changing World

Prof Jim Lucey

HACHETTE
BOOKS
IRELAND

Copyright © 2021 Jim Lucey

The right of Jim Lucey to be identified as the Author of
the Work has been asserted by him in accordance with the
Copyright, Designs and Patents Act 1988.

First published in Ireland in 2021 by
HACHETTE BOOKS IRELAND

2

All rights reserved. No part of this publication may be reproduced, stored in
a retrieval system, or transmitted, in any form or by any means without the
prior written permission of the publisher, nor be otherwise circulated in any
form of binding or cover other than that in which it is published and without
a similar condition being imposed on the subsequent purchaser.

Cataloguing in Publication Data is available from the British Library

ISBN 9781529345650

Typeset in Sabon by redrattledesign.com
Image p.77: Pyty/shutterstock.com
All other images: Cathal O'Gara

Printed and bound in Great Britain by
Clays, Elcograf S.p.A.

Hachette Books Ireland policy is to use papers that are natural, renewable
and recyclable products and made from wood grown in sustainable forests.
The logging and manufacturing processes are expected to conform to the
environmental regulations of the country of origin.

Hachette Books Ireland
8 Castlecourt Centre
Castleknock
Dublin 15, Ireland

A division of Hachette UK Ltd
Carmelite House, 50 Victoria Embankment, EC4Y 0DZ

www.hachettebooksireland.ie

For those we have lost
Sursum corda (Lift up your hearts)

'I balanced all, brought all to mind,
The years to come seemed waste of breath,
A waste of breath the years behind,
In balance with this life, this death.'

'*An Irish Airman Foresees His Death*' – W.B. Yeats

Contents

Introduction: Beginning Your Whole New Plan   1

Step One: Understanding Wellness   18

Step Two: Establishing Paths to Wellbeing   34

Step Three: Finding Ways to Greater Emotional Wellbeing   62

Step Four: Maintaining Health and Wellness in Difficult Times   75

Step Five: Recognising a Mentally Healthy Life   117

Step Six: Making This Plan Your Own   141

Step Seven: Recognising the Social Determinants of Health   156

Step Eight: Moving from Stress and Distress to Recovery   188

Step Nine: Tools for Your Whole New Plan   225

Step Ten: What to do When Balance is Lost   238

Epilogue   277

Acknowledgements   281

Bibliography   283

Endnotes   285

Index 292

Introduction

Beginning Your Whole New Plan

This book is about our shared search for wellness, and my hope is that it will help very many people. Some of us have been going through more hardship than others, but all of us have been looking for greater equilibrium in a world which seems so uncertain. Several people have asked me to recommend them an authentic guide to better health – one that is clearer and more helpful than before, something that is sensible, scientific and well informed. In the end I decided to write such a guide for myself, and this book is the result. It is about the pursuit of a better way of living. There have been many past attempts to define what it means to be well, but in this book we will consider *how* to be well, and how to achieve this in the here and now.

I also hope that this will be an uplifting, motivating and empowering book. While all of us seek a healthier way of living, perhaps because of my experience as a psychiatrist I have my own perspective on the issue. It is this: I believe the key to the search for wellness is the search for better mental health. Central to our experience of wellbeing is the achievement of 'balance', and so the hallmark of a healthy life is balanced mental health.

We will all experience challenging times in our lives – everyone goes through some distress and none of us is immune to the difficulties of living. Still, I believe that every human being has a right to live a mentally healthy life, and so somehow, we all need to learn how to take better care of ourselves and of each other. To do this we need a whole new plan for living. This new plan is about acquiring the tools to be well and increasing the skills we need to stay well, especially when we become distressed. In this book we will explore some of these skills, skills that will help us – each reader and myself included – to describe our own whole new plan for living. Awareness of the skills for wellness will help us to balance the stress we experience with the opportunities for health that we share.

That's not to say that there is only one way to live well – it's not my intention to direct anyone to live by some ordained route. When it comes to living a well and healthy life, there is no North Star, no guide for everyone to navigate the same way. But there are some skills and tools which, if applied, could lead any human being to greater contentment. I do not intend to limit your new plan for healthy living, rather I hope to empower you to make your own, personal plan, one that is most likely to give you the healthy life you are entitled to.

One in every six of us will have a mental health disorder this year.[i] All the common mental health difficulties have been exacerbated by the global COVID-19 pandemic, which has plunged the world into a state of emergency and panic. At least one member of every family is in mental distress at this very moment, and for those at the extreme end of that distress, suicide has become the most common cause of death under the age of fifty. None of this is inevitable; all of this could change. We could learn to take better care of ourselves, to worry less and to forgive more. This is not a utopian ideal – with a whole new plan for living we could learn to live with each other in a more balanced, robust and resilient fashion.

Three skill sets will come up again and again as we work together to make a whole new plan for living. These principal tools are:

- The eight dimensions of health[ii]
- 'CHIME' – the five features of recovery[iii]
- The five ways to wellness[iv]

No one alive today can deny how challenging life has become. Of course, life has never been fair or easy, but in the twenty-first century life does not need to be 'nasty, brutish and short', as English philosopher Thomas Hobbes once described it. It could also be wonderful, surprising and rewarding in ways we never imagined. This more hopeful, resilient vision is justified by my experience of mental health recovery, and this witness of recovery is still true even after a long career and many a health crisis. With a whole new plan for living it will be possible to turn the growing awareness of our difficulty into greater action for our recovery. This action will require a much better understanding of our health, and this will give us more hope, more compassion and a greater ability to take care of ourselves.

To achieve this understanding, we need to learn more about our health and its complexity. Good health is complex, and so the solutions to our recovery will also be. Our health is not one-dimensional; in fact, it has at least eight dimensions. Despite this complexity, better health is not a difficult concept to grasp. I like to compare good health to a bright star in the sky: as we imagine better health in this way, we will begin to see its glowing shape. As we travel towards this star, we will see it shine and appreciate its many sides. The good news is that better health is much nearer than the stars.

The sides of this glowing star, this healthy polygon, reflect the eight dimensions of wellness or what we will refer to as the whole of health (as outlined by the Substance Abuse and Mental Health Services Administration or SAMHSA):

1. Physical

2. Financial

3. Occupational

4. Environmental

5. Intellectual

6. Social

7. Emotional

8. Spiritual

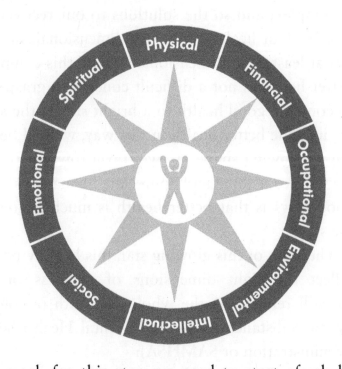

To reach for this star, we need to start afresh by talking more positively about our goals and our targets. We need to re-harness our means and rethink our new strategy. We need to move our health conversation from a past filled with pessimism to a new and more hopeful place.

We do not need to be resigned about our existing health: better health is something we can plan for. Through research we have come to know what makes one healthcare initiative work and another fail. The characteristics of any successful recovery plan have been well described and they are best remembered using the acronym CHIME, a shorthand for the features of healthy recovery:

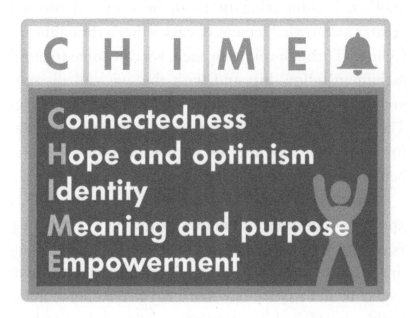

CHIME is a good description of what works. Many years of experience in healthcare have taught me that our plans for our health are more likely to succeed if they CHIME! We will talk more about the elements of CHIME in Step Eight of our whole new plan (page 201).

None of this will happen in a vacuum: the environment for better health begins with better communication. It is facilitated by what I call 'the listening conversation'. By making this healthy dialogue part of our everyday lives, we will give the communication of our health the priority it deserves. Listening conversation is different from the 'nod and wink' conversation we are so used to. It means hearing each other and growing in understanding of one another, a connection that can be achieved through greater acknowledgement of each other's thoughts and feelings. Through this approach, we can come together in human fellowship and with this we will discover greater compassion for ourselves and for each other. There is no single right way to live, but a better plan for living will connect us with each other in many better ways.

During the Great Recession that began in 2008, a group of economists affiliated to the New Economics Foundation (NEF) took up the challenge of describing the ways to greater wellness. For centuries those in medicine and psychology had struggled to agree about health and failed to put into easily understandable words the essence of what it is to be well. Some of the ancient classical scholars described 'the life well lived' and talked about 'the healthy mind in the healthy body', but a modern, practical understanding of what healthy living really looks like eluded us for thousands of years. In the nineteenth century, the psychoanalysts came closer when they described good health as the ability to live, to work and to love. Still, the detail of wellness has never been clear enough. Even now in this age of information overload, we are still not sure what it means to be well. So, the NEF economists came back with their answer: 'the five ways to wellness' – the characteristic ways of being well. These are behaviours seen in people who describe themselves as well and who actually live healthy everyday, ordinary lives. Healthy people characteristically do these five things:

* They connect with each other.

* They keep active.

* They take notice.

* They keep learning.

* They give.

We will talk about these in more detail later in the book, but for now I will say that my favourite of the five ways to wellness is 'giving'. This 'giving' is not just the charitable giving that is so familiar to us. There is no doubting the value of giving to charity, but the healthy giving of wellness is much greater than this. This healthy way to live is by giving to each of us. Giving is a form of self-love and it is a life-giving therapy for each person. It's about learning to give way. Learning to give ground. Learning to give credit to ourselves and to give that credit to others in whole new ways. An inanimate object such as a table or a chair has little 'give'. If enough pressure is put upon such an object, the only outcome is that it will break, simply because the object has no flexibility, no give, within it. Human beings, on the other hand, have flexibility – we can learn how to adapt, and so with our elastic capacity for 'give' we can prepare for whatever life throws at us. Well people already understand this. They give themselves more time and they give themselves more space. Essentially their giving is a kind of love. By starting to give this love to themselves they recover and go on to find love in their surroundings and in each other. In health we learn that kindness to ourselves and to others balances most things and so it restores us to wellbeing.

Life is still a struggle for most of us. Psychologists tell us that we live in a world characterised by the acronym VUCA: a world that is volatile, uncertain, complex and ambiguous. Our VUCA world cannot simply be ignored or denied. A VUCA world must be engaged with, so we need a strategic plan. A volatile world needs greater balance – it will not just settle for us. An uncertain world needs more than one certainty, which is the inevitability of further change. Our complex world needs more than one simple truth, which is that we are all struggling, and so from our ambiguous world we need to form a whole new plan for a more balanced, healthy life.

These three healthy principles – the eight dimensions of health, five ways to wellness and CHIME – will be well described in this book but my interest in them is more personal than you might imagine. Let me tell you why.

I first came across the idea of a whole new plan for living in a conversation with someone who was very ill. He was an elderly man with a very serious health problem, and it was my task to tell him the final news of his diagnosis. As I gave him the sad truth, he listened to me very carefully, and then after a long pause, he began to speak to me.

'If what you're telling me about my health is true, Jim,' he said, 'then there is something I want you to do for me.'

'Of course,' I replied. 'What do you want me to do?'

'I want you to give me a whole new plan for living.'

This elderly man was my late father and we were talking about his last illness. In the middle of this conversation about his death, he encouraged me to talk to him about life, and about a whole new plan for living.

I remember thinking to myself, 'How can I give him a whole new plan? I don't have any such plan. I certainly can't prescribe a plan ...'

But the more I thought about it, the more I realised that a whole new plan for living was exactly what we both needed. He might have added the phrase, carpe diem (seize the day) but now I know that his point was greater than this cliché. In responding to me he was doing more than stressing the urgency of a plan for his treatment, he was encouraging me to believe in the hope of living.

Why shouldn't we make our plan for living? Why shouldn't we do this now, at this stage of our lives? There never was a successful initiative without a great plan. Surely now we must realise that there is no point in postponement. Something so important as our health should not be delayed or left to chance. It is a mark of our right to human autonomy that we each take responsibility for our health. And so our whole new plan for living could be based on a more balanced understanding, one that is grounded in a combination of science, experience and common sense.

When we acknowledge our need for such a plan, we do this not only for ourselves, but for our world too. Now more than ever we need new ways of thinking about the whole of our health, including our environmental health and our mental health. 20 per cent of the people presenting to general practice have a mental health difficulty[v] and worldwide one in every ten adults has a mental health disorder.[vi] Our greatest unmet needs involve the mind. The way forward does not have to be random or muddled, even if our lives are complex. Healthy living can come about if we learn and make changes, finding new ways to recover together, and for this we will need a whole new plan.

Developing a healthy plan will take some time, but taking this time is good. We all prefer the promise of quick fixes, of easy ways and easy solutions, but these often-promised shortcuts to wellness are inauthentic because they leave out one essential ingredient – time.

In planning for our healthy living, we will embrace time and do this mindfully, regardless of how little we may have of it left. It is a mistake to regard time as our enemy – time spent on making a whole new plan will always be time well spent; a more mindful understanding of our time will allow us to acknowledge its passing now. This mindfulness is not a form of denial, it is a healthier understanding of time and health. To love time more, we must feel it now, and then let it go. This is true at every stage and for everything in life, even near its very end. This mindful gift of time is one of the many paradoxes in a healthier, more balanced life. Planning with time means accepting that so much of our hoped-for experience is transient. Everything passes, and so planning for a better life means recognising that this life is always passing. That is the beauty of it. Planning with time is the most mindful experience of all.

Each day, we face new and unforeseen challenges – to our health, our life and our habitats. The old ways of living and working will no longer meet our current needs and so we cannot wait for others to come up with new solutions. If we do not plan for this change for ourselves, we will become more anxious and more distressed. We must plan for new ways to be well, to be social, to be collective and to be productive.

In my own life, I have experienced many changes, including retirement from a busy leadership role, transition to a more clinical one, and other inevitable changes in my health and in my family life. These events have brought me back emotionally to my late father's last instruction to me, 'make a whole new plan for living', and so I have been re-evaluating things.

Hopefully through this book we will help each other to discover our whole new plan for living, a plan that is so necessary for each of us at this time. We will start by acknowledging the challenge. This plan will not be a final or a complete notion of our health, but it will be a fresh start. Healthy living for each of us has become a more varied and more dynamic challenge, and so our new plan will be about living in a better present and preparing for a better tomorrow. Every one of us has a right to hope for a better future, and the key to that better future is a whole new plan for health and wellness today.

In order for our plan to work, we will need to achieve greater balance in our lives, with increased harmony between our abilities and our disabilities. We will need to live a life with more equilibrium – a healthier life is one that respects our human identity and values our social experience. Our whole new plan will include a renewed respect for the unique narrative of our lives, for who we are and where we come from, for how we love and how we live. It is about building upon our ability to live with ourselves and to live with each other at the same time in an ever more crowded world. It's time for a whole new plan for living and so I hope that we will begin to make it today.

Moving from contemplation to action: Your blank page

Throughout this book I will be encouraging you to take practical steps for your health and wellness. Some of these steps will be easier than others, and so a great deal depends on how you feel. Do not worry. Remember that you can always come back to an earlier step and benefit from it. Take your time. Each step will have its pros and its cons. As we proceed, we will be considering in more detail some issues (of health and wellness). Some are hidden in the background and others are revealed in the foreground and are emerging throughout the whole of life. Any successful strategic venture will need some periods of thought and some extra moments for greater preparation. There will always be things for you to consider before taking any particular step, and even then there will be moments when you will need to reconsider how you will proceed, but making a strategic plan for our health is a process in itself. As we go ahead, we will take into account aspects of our shared experience and also our reading of the scientific data.

Maybe, like me, you have been considering a way forward for some time, but just not getting around to it. It doesn't matter; this time will be different because this is the right time. We must not chastise ourselves – there have always been false starts. A period of increasing awareness is essential before any successful action begins. This period before the plan is called the 'pre-contemplation phase'. During this time, a bolder set of decisions grows within us and in time the detail of our decisions becomes apparent, leading us to the next era known as the 'contemplation phase'. Pre-contemplation and contemplation are both necessary. In the eyes of others, nothing has happened, and yet we know that an important part of the work has begun. Now we are ready to take the first steps for our wellbeing.

I hope you have decided to make your whole new plan for living. This decision to begin is the most important step of all. It's time to make a start, and to do it simply, by placing a blank piece of paper and a pencil before you. This is where your whole new plan will be written; you will write it on this blank page, equipped with only a hopeful heart and an open mind. This is all you need for now. It's time to begin.

Step One

Understanding Wellness

We have made a good start. We have begun our whole new plan for living exactly where we should, with an open mind, a hopeful heart, a pencil, and a blank piece of paper. Our whole new plan will be like all the best strategies, a fresh gathering of all our resources in order to meet our new goal. It is a fundamental premise of this book that wellness and recovery is that goal. But what do we mean by 'wellness'? And what is good health?

Good health is about so much more than the absence of disease. It is about a balance in all things, physical and mental. It has many sides to it and each of these sides has an effect on another. To achieve better health, we will need to do many new things, taking several actions, knowing that each of these steps will only have a small effect on the whole of our health. Making this strategy work will take patience, but putting together as many of these healthy actions as possible in order to maximise our wellbeing is the business of planning a new, healthier life. This business is as complex as it is urgent and that is why it requires our attention now. Hence the need for our whole new plan for living.

Achieving better health is a balancing act. Our new plan will recognise our need for greater equilibrium by addressing our human health in a much broader, more poised way than ever before. Seen in this way, our health becomes something to be nurtured, sustained and balanced. We do not need to be afraid of this new wellness agenda just because it is something complex and finely balanced. Like life itself, the factors of human health are diverse and dynamic.

I like to compare the pursuit of health and wellness to the experience of working in a circus. I have never worked in a circus, but I remember the thrill that I felt as a small boy when the local circus would come to town. Looking back now I can see that our circus was nothing fancy or extraordinary. There were no wild animals or big trapeze acts. The performers made do with a couple of piebald horses, some clowns and a fire eater, but I loved our circus and I never noticed in all my wonder that the clown who made me laugh at the interval was the same person who took my ticket at the gate. It never occurred to me that the circus master and the cast appeared in many different guises and performed many other roles. So why do I imagine life as being a bit like the circus? Because it is a universal, timeless and yet complex experience in which each person must play many different parts.

I remember one act in particular. I used to call it 'the man spinning plates'. For whatever reason this memory has become one of my recurring dreams. In my dream the circus plate-spinner is dressed in a long-tailed sparkling suit and he amazes us all, first by spinning one, then two and, a little later, more than ten china plates, each at first spinning and then some teetering, upon tall sticks arranged in a circle around him. Inevitably the plates become unbalanced, and one by one they begin to crash and fall. Just then, reassuringly, his 'lovely assistant' enters the ring. Gracefully she restores the balancing act to its equilibrium. Together they keep the plates spinning till a fanfare calls the whole performance to a pleasing halt. Clearly this is my fantasy! But within this dream lies the reality of our lives; that they are full of challenges, and just like spinning plates, it is not easy to balance all of these at the same time.

That is why my favourite definition of health is the multidimensional one, known as 'the eight dimensions of health'. We might think of each of these dimensions as a spinning plate. Each is carrying an important aspect of healthy living. This model of wellbeing comes from the US Substance Abuse and Mental Health Services Administration (SAMHSA). As explained on page 5, the eight dimensions of health are: physical, financial, occupational, environmental, intellectual, social, emotional and spiritual. It is important to understand that no one can keep all these 'plates' spinning at the same time without some help, but together these eight dimensions capture the complexity and the equipoise, the richness and the potential, of a healthy life. Any one dimension may be present or absent, plentiful or scarce, each may spin or fall, but the sum of them is a positive value we call 'health'. That is why health is not just the absence of something else. Health is about the balance of many things.

Let's take a closer look at each of the eight dimensions of health and consider in more detail how they might form a basis for our whole new plan for living.

1. Physical health

Physical health is the aspect of health we are most familiar with. This refers to 'fitness' and it benefits from good self-care, from our attention to our diet and exercise and from better sleep. We will be discussing all these things a little later, but for now I want to put this idea of physical health into some context. One of the

most dangerous misunderstandings of health comes from what is known as the 'dualist definition'. This error sees our health as consisting of just two things: 'a healthy mind in a healthy body'. Nowadays we know that this is an error because we know there is no division between our physical health and our mental wellbeing. Each part of health is dependent upon the other. Physical health refers to our bodily integrity, and the practical expression of this is a greater concern for exercise, diet and relaxation. Better physical health results from a more energetic participation in these activities and these help to maintain our general wellbeing.

Some people see the pursuit of this physical health as the route to the entirety of their wellness, but it is not. Physical health cannot exist on its own. It is only sustained when we take better care of ourselves in a 'whole' sense. That is why our new plan is called 'a whole new plan for living'. When it comes to physical health, we begin to do this 'whole' caring by looking after the balance of our lives, our work and our play, by getting enough exercise and relaxation, and by taking reasonable steps to maintain our safety from other hazards (such as alcohol and tobacco).

Even then there is more to our physical health than all of this; to be physically well we must be able to endure many things, to be better able to cope with episodes of disorder (caused by stress, trauma or depression) and at

times even a certain level of disease (such as those caused by diabetes or cancers). As we grow older, we are more likely to be living with one or more enduring physical illnesses (for example high blood pressure or arthritis) and yet, despite all of these, we can still be physically healthy. The challenge of living well with illness makes physical health more of a priority and not less.

2. Financial health

Financial health is also commonly misunderstood. It's a mistake to measure our personal health in terms of our absolute personal wealth. While all of us worry about money from time to time and we all feel anxious about our debts, the key to financial wellbeing lies in having the balance right.

Some things about financial health are absolute – for example, outright poverty is never good for health. Every disease known to human beings has a worse effect on the poor. Sickness is amplified by financial jeopardy and it is sustained by poverty. According to the sociologist Sir Michael Marmot, we need to acknowledge 'the social determinants of ill-health and disease': the poor always have more suffering, more disease and, inevitably, shorter lives. Consequently, financial health cannot be dismissed as simply a tangent to the whole of a healthy life.[vii] Our financial wellbeing is central to the whole of our health. Our new plan for living will include a recognition of this fact.

But there is no absolute level of income we should aspire to that is synonymous with good health. The bonus culture that preceded the 2008 recession revealed the folly of monetary rewards as a route to better health. After a certain amount of financial incentive our true financial health becomes subjective. It is true that poverty can make us ill, but after a certain point more money does not make us happier or healthier. Once again, like all the other dimensions of health, financial health lies in the balance. 'Enough is as good as a feast', as they used to say. Whether more money brings us satisfaction is personally linked to our sense of satisfaction with our current circumstances and with our prospects. Financial health is therefore a moving target. It shifts with our environment and varies with our responsibilities. Financial health is not static, and so like stocks and shares, it too can rise and fall with sentiment.

3. Occupational health

Working should be good for us; a productive life is more likely to be a healthy one. Occupational health is one of the clearest illustrations of balance within our wellbeing. Too much work is just as harmful as too little. Good occupational health comes from a sense of personal satisfaction that results from doing a job well. Working in this way gives us a sense of purpose, identity and reward. It also gives us a daily routine, a structure and a sense of achievement. In many settings, work brings people closer to other people, both physically and psychologically, by sharing in a sense of purpose.

There are some who give too much priority to their work or have too big a workload; both burdens can lead to greater work stress and an increased risk of burnout. Occupational burnout is characterised by a diminished sense of respect for the work as well as reduced energy and a poorer quality of performance. Burnout can affect anyone in the workplace, especially if enough stress is placed upon someone, but it is most frequently identified in people such as first responders, healthcare workers and teachers after long exposure to extreme levels of stress.

Some workplaces are more hazardous than others. The risks range from physical dangers, to more social and interpersonal ones. The latter include discrimination, bullying and sexual or racial harassment. Working in such environments rapidly becomes an unhealthy and unrewarding pursuit. A healthy workplace is one that values its workers and ensures their protection from exploitation, and it's also one that recognises the balance of work and personal life. Nevertheless, around the world growing numbers of people, mostly women and children, are trapped in poor working conditions, some approaching modern-day slavery. Industry of this kind cannot be healthy. It is an abuse of the right to a dignified and rewarding workplace, a disregard for workers' occupational health and a deprivation of their fundamental rights or freedoms.

In a healthy society occupational health becomes a two-way street where we must value our work and our work must value us. Work should be good for our health. In our new plan for our health we will re-evaluate our work and our workplaces and put a greater premium on their health-giving capacities.

4. Environmental health

This is the dimension of health that derives from the context of our lives and the quality of the spaces in which we live. These include the spaces around us, the spaces between us and the spaces within us. The quality of each of these environments is crucial to healthy living. In making our whole new plan for living we will spend some more time considering each of these areas, the extra-personal space, which we might call our 'milieu', as well as the interpersonal and the intrapersonal spaces in which we live and work. A pleasant and satisfying habitat is more likely to be good for the health of any living creature and the same is true for our human wellbeing. Many people find the quality of their mood is closely linked to the quality of their surroundings, so they find joy in living and working in a stimulating, safe and harmonious environment. Living or working in places that are threatening, violent or dirty is bound to be harmful to anyone. Many people live in environments which are neither safe nor satisfying.

We may have little or no agency over our external environment. We may do our best at an individual level, but few of us can choose to live in a better neighbourhood or to breathe in cleaner air. So, what can we do to make a meaningful contribution to our environmental health? The answer is to be found in the balance of things. As we have already agreed, active concern for a healthy environment includes taking responsibility for the spaces within us as well as the spaces between us and the wider environment around us. Our whole new plan could be a new strategic way of thinking about these shared environmental spaces and an opportunity to make changes for our better health.

5. Intellectual health

Improving this aspect of our health involves the discovery of our unique creative ability. By promoting this we will find new routes to greater health, new routes to fulfilment, and renewed sources of meaning and empowerment in our lives. So how might our whole new plan for living increase our intellectual health? The answer is by expanding our access to learning and creativity. This may not be easy for some, since access to more creativity is not equal in our society.

Also, many of us are shy about this creative aspect of our lives, not feeling confident about our ability to make and do. But creativity can be about small tasks or larger ones. It's not about achieving all our creative goals but about enjoying the moment of their pursuit. Making our whole new plan will be an opportunity to awaken within us some of our creative instincts and to experience the enjoyment of things that we may have left behind since childhood.

So, when it comes to our intellectual health let's ask ourselves today what was it that we 'used to do'? We may find that we 'used to' write or we 'used to' draw or paint or knit, or make this or that, but today on reflection we realise that we no longer do these things. We may even have come to believe that we are not able to do these things anymore. In our whole new plan, we will turn these 'used to dos' into our 'will dos' and by recovering our creativity we will enhance our intellectual health. We will learn that our health is not just about going to the gym, or eating a better diet, or getting better sleep (even though all these things are important). Taking time to promote our creative skills and even to discover new ones could be a very important part of our whole new plan for living.

6. Social health

We are social creatures. To a greater or lesser degree, we form collectives, we make families, villages, towns and cities, and even nations. We do this 'social' stuff because we are human and so we benefit from coming together. Social health is the dimension of our wellness that recognises the importance of our human connectedness. Rediscovering this aspect of our health is one of the most important aspects of recovery. It's the first letter of our recovery acronym CHIME: the 'c' is for connecting. Enhancing our social health means rebuilding and maintaining our social networks, whether this is with family and friends, colleagues or neighbours. Our social system is a priceless health resource. Whether this includes involvement with clubs or support groups, a well-developed social connection is an invaluable dimension of our health and it is a great source of our resilient strength.

Our whole new plan for living will include a re-examination of our social network. Let's ask ourselves a few questions about our social wellbeing. How connected are we? Are these connections close or distant? How can we improve our connectedness? Where is our community? Whether it is at home, down the road or online, a sense of being connected to a community of others is an invaluable aspect of our health.

The first step to enhancing social health is to value our connections to each other. Every known route to wellness emphasises the value of human connectedness. The five ways to wellness begin with encouragement to 'connect', because those who are well connect with each other. Reconnection within ourselves and within our community is not just a challenge for our health but a reliable route to our recovery. Although this connectedness may be lost in illness, it is restored in health. As with the other dimensions of wellbeing, social reconnecting is not easy for everyone. Some of us find social connectedness extremely difficult, experiencing everything from mild shyness to extreme forms of social phobia. Nonetheless, it remains true that by restoring and sustaining our social network, we add an important dimension to the whole of our health. Reconnecting could be one of the most valuable health initiatives in our whole new plan.

7. Emotional health

Emotional health is often misunderstood. Emotions are the innermost expressions of our moods and they are naturally fluctuant. Like the tides, our emotions must ebb and flow, and inevitably they rise and fall. Emotional wellbeing is the dimension of health that travels with us and so it sustains warm and constructive relationships, despite its tidal behaviour. Emotional balance or 'equanimity' promotes personal calmness, and this gives us the ability to remain composed under stress, to tolerate the tidal feelings within us as well the jagged sensitivities between us.

Emotional sensitivity varies between people. Some

people can tolerate intense emotional feelings with greater ease than others, and some can step over emotional difficulties that many others simply could not cross. Better emotional health allows us to bridge these gaps. Emotional health is a resilient resource that is both personal and interpersonal. It sustains our innermost wellbeing and the health of our relationships.

Emotional health has a lot to do with temperament but, like every other aspect of health, it can be learned and enhanced to some degree. Acquiring this strength means having greater capacity to tolerate stressful fluctuations in our feelings and so to regulate these feelings over the most difficult times. Achieving this emotional balance is more difficult for some than it is for others, and so this is a form of learning that always takes time. To paraphrase Marsha Linehan, the originator of 'Dialectical Behaviour Therapy',[viii] better health is about learning to balance our 'emotional mind' and our 'wise mind'. It is not static – emotional health can increase with life experience or be interrupted by life distress. Our whole new plan for living will recognise and value our emotional health.

8. Spiritual health

Of course, it is possible to be healthy without being spiritual, but just like every other healthy dimension, our spiritual health is in balance with the other seven.[ix]

No one spins every healthy plate at the same time, and so no single dimension of health has complete dominance over any other.

This spiritual health has very little to do with religion. The eighteenth-century Irish satirist Jonathan Swift may have put this best when he said, 'We have enough religion to make us hate, but not enough to make us love one another.' Spirituality is generally good for health; religion may or may not be. That is why whenever I raise the subject of spirituality in my clinic, I do so very cautiously. Many people are indifferent to the issue; others are quick to dismiss the idea of spiritual health along with aspects of organised religion; but some respond to my enquiry with interest by saying that while they do not consider themselves religious, they do like to consider themselves to be spiritual. So, is this spirituality good for your health?

Spirituality within an organised religion brings people into greater fellowship with others who share a faith. Religious fellowship of this kind may be healthy, especially if the affiliation is one of deep commitment. It remains a challenge to distinguish the benefits of spirituality from those of committed religious affiliation, except to say that the greatest benefits of spiritual health also come to those who take their spirit seriously, regardless of their denomination. This reality of spiritual health might be challenging for those without a specific faith, but it shouldn't be. We do not need to be afraid of spirituality.

Putting this more simply, it's the quality of any spiritual dimension in our life that matters, not the way we identify it. Spiritual relationships are like any other kind, at least in this regard; when they are more engaged, more sincere, and more sustained, they are better for us. So, spirituality gives some people access to another form of relationship that supports them. This spiritual access is completely egalitarian; perhaps that's why people today like it so much. Identifying our personal spiritual access is as important as any of the other aspects of our whole new plan for living.

Step Two

Establishing Paths to Wellbeing

It's time to consider taking the second step of our whole new plan. We have considered the whole of our health and its many dimensions; now we need some specifics. And in order to sustain our long-term efforts we need to see some quick results. Every plan needs some early successes, some relatively easy wins, before we approach even more challenging stuff later. It's important to see better health as a diverse mix, something made up of many minor ingredients, each with a small effect on 'the whole'. I imagine it's like making a soup; in time all the ingredients will combine to make a better soup, but this is not the time to chastise ourselves for the omission of one or another part.

The early changes we can make to our behaviour are our strategy's building blocks – better eating, sleeping and exercise. Laying a foundation in these areas will provide us with some solid progress, and this will be enough to keep us on the right road, while at the same time helping us to reduce any inflammation that we experience when we are distressed. Subsequent actions taken as part of our whole new plan for our health will be more effective if we have already addressed these everyday ways to wellbeing.

So, let's consider Step Two of our new plan in more detail. In everyday life some universal challenges must arise. That is why my patients often ask me questions like, 'How should I eat?', 'How can I get better sleep?', 'What should I be doing to help myself stay calm?' These questions deserve to be heard and answered. These answers are informed by the scientific data and by experience and by practicality. Step Two includes taking actions around four practical issues in everyday life that we all need to address:

1. Eating

2. Sleeping

3. Exercising

4. Reducing inflammation

How to eat

I have never found it easy to give or to take dietary advice. Instructions to eat more of this healthy food or less of that unhealthy one just put me off. Making a whole new plan for healthy living is not supposed to be a didactic experience. This is, after all, your plan, so in a way it must be your menu. I don't believe in chastisement in therapy, and my experience tells me that planning for living well will only succeed if we form a better partnership for health. This partnership is within us and with other people and it must be built upon trust.[x] It's not enhanced by being told what to do or what to eat. The many challenges that we have experienced together through the COVID-19 pandemic have made the need for a more trusted partnership in health even more obvious and more important. Making our whole new plan for living now provides a fresh opportunity to reconsider our health together and to put our plans into action.

Food is personal. I like my food – and I hope that you do too – but, like many other people, I try to convince myself that I know just enough of the dietary basics to stay well. I am familiar with the usual advice about taking five fruit or vegetables a day and ensuring a good balance of the main food groups. Still, I occasionally ask myself 'What am I doing?' So, when people ask me to recommend a particular diet to them, they want to know which foods will help them to resolve their symptoms of stress and distress. Like every aspect of healthy living, the truthful answer is not straightforward. To my knowledge, there isn't one single diet that can make us well. Healthy eating is important, but it's just not that simple.

Many people around the world eat a staple diet. This is one based upon a single source of nourishment like rice or cornmeal, possibly with some fish. Many others live in terrible want and try to survive despite long periods of hunger, but in the Western world, food supply has largely been secure for more than fifty years.

Today, we can eat foods regardless of season, distance travelled or country of origin. We have access to better information about food production methods, diet and nutrition, and we are learning to understand that we needn't take all the marketing claims about food products at face value. Healthy eating has become as much about how we eat as what we eat.

A healthy eating plan recognises that the anti-stress aspects of mindful eating are mostly social and cultural, and so the search for a better way to eat starts with a few questions.

* How do you feel about preparing food?

* Do you use processed food, or can you use raw materials when making a meal?

* Do you like to eat alone or with others?

* Are there any other personal factors that
influence the way you eat?

To find the best and healthiest way of eating for our
whole new plan for living, we need to keep in mind the
eight dimensions of health and the five ways to wellness
(see pages 5 and 9). We need to know the facts of our
mental health and to reconsider our dietary habits in
the context of greater recovery in our own lives. The
answers to our food questions are therefore not so
much dietary. Good eating is like all the other aspects
of our healthy new plan: it is about achieving a more
balanced experience.

Preparation of food, like the anticipation of it, can
bring us great pleasure, and even greater relief from
stress. Unfortunately, the urgent drive within our
culture over the past fifty years has been towards faster
and faster food, making speed of access to food more
important than our enjoyment of it. Home delivery
of prepared meals and pre-packaged instant meals
have become commonplace. Indeed, at times they are
an essential 'meals on wheels' type service. I am not
debating whether these should be widely available. I
am recommending that we become more able to value
and experience the enjoyment of anticipating and
preparing food. Healthy eating includes the sharing
and savouring of these moments.

The increasing rapidity of our consumption has
coincided with an increase in our preoccupation with

prepared food. Bookshelves and television programmes are full of items about cooking. Dietary publications and colourful cookery shows appear in many attractive guises. We may have less time to eat our food, but we are spending more time than ever on our interest in it. It is good that our food supply is more diverse in origin, but now could be the time to restore what we have lost in our food – time spent collecting, preparing, eating and sharing it. Rediscovering our good food time could be a healthy part of our whole new plan for living.

This is not meant as some nostalgic vision; I am not recommending that we return to the precarious life of our hunter-gatherer ancestors. The hungry burden of millions of people around the world whose day is spent gathering and preparing staple foods is an enslaved struggle that no one would recommend. What I am saying is that in our age of seemingly endless supply, we have lost something else.

So, regarding our food, which healthy changes should we include in our whole new plan for living? Remember that Step Two of our plan is about making changes to our everyday lives in the interest of our wellbeing, so each of us will need to decide what works for us. We might decide to prepare more of our meals for ourselves, even if we start with this once a week. If we can source unprocessed foodstuffs and have access to a kitchen, we could take more time to prepare our food. The homeless, those living in direct provision and those on the margins cannot do this, but many of us who have the means would benefit from re-learning how to bake or prepare a stew or a roast. We could try to grow more of our vegetables. Nurturing a garden or a window box can bring about a significant lift in our mood. That is why allotment use, community gardens and vegetable-growing are on the increase. This observation is common in many popular food books and in the growing numbers of TV programmes about diet and gardening, suggesting that, at least in our unconscious minds, we know that greater time spent preparing and nurturing food would be a source of renewed mental peace.

Eating in a more mindful, conscious way – enjoying the taste and smell of our food and savouring this experience in the moment – would make our diet an even healthier part of our lives. This more conscious way of eating would make this process a greater part of our connection with our human nature and with other people.

Another benefit of taking more time over our food is that it is more hygienic, and less open to contamination. The transfer of infections (from viruses and prions – infective agents) into our food chain caused some of the biggest health emergencies in modern times. This contamination was caused, on the one hand, by the pressure to produce larger volumes more quickly and, on the other hand, by a reduced consciousness of the natural boundaries essential for the production of safe food. Responsibility for this disregard lies on the shoulders of leaders and legislators more than on individual farmers or consumers, but much has been learned from the emergence of a brain disease called bovine spongiform encephalopathy, or 'mad cow disease'. This was caused by feeding animal brain proteins (containing prions) to naturally herbivorous creatures. The additional weight on the cattle proved valuable at the market, but the profits were short-lived for society. Vast numbers of cattle had to be destroyed in order to clean the food chain of prion infection. Mindless food production is hazardous, and the damage can be long-term.

The recent COVID-19 pandemic was caused by a process known as 'zoonosis', in which a viral infection normally residing in animals transfers to human beings, where it becomes even more toxic. Coronaviruses were previously limited to reptiles and bats, but this one appears to have been transferred to human beings via the food chain. Creatures infected with this virus were either eaten by humans or bought and sold in markets close to other human foods. Whatever emerges from the investigation of the causes of the COVID-19 pandemic, it's clear that the restoration of confidence in the integrity and safety of our food production will be vital.

Our food production needs to have greater respect for the basic boundaries between food groups. A greater collective cultural understanding of these boundaries is important in times of globalisation. None of this wisdom is new, but our worries regarding the integrity of our food are likely to become a greater source of twenty-first-century anxiety.

As the world's population grows, so will our food safety concerns. The dilemma of how to access safe food for so many will only increase. In order to provide safe food for more than seven billion people living on Earth, this responsibility for the sustainability of a secure food supply needs to become a shared human concern. This is not a hypothetical issue. Many people have difficulty accessing safe food fit for preparation.

By eating more mindfully, as part of our whole new plan for living, we would be taking one step to address these food security and safety issues. Eating in a more balanced way could become part of a restored connection with each other and with our environment. Eating mindfully is not just about enjoying the taste and smell of our food. It's about being able to trust its integrity while enjoying the moment of eating it and experiencing the moment for what it is. We have prepared the food. We have anticipated it. Now it's time to savour it.

Considered in this way, our diet's value is not just its calorific level. Our food also matters because of the way it looks, feels, tastes and smells. Food fills our senses as much as our stomachs. A whole new way of eating in a more balanced way will help us to feel less stressed and to live well.

So that is probably why so many people ask me, 'What is the healthiest diet?' If I had to pick one type, I would choose the Mediterranean diet. This is a diet based on the eating pattern once typical of the Mediterranean coast of southern Italy and Greece. It's a diet abundant in fresh fruits, vegetables and wholegrains, legumes and olive oil. It includes eggs and cheese, pasta and bread, lean meat, fish and poultry. Red meat is kept to a minimum but red wine is allowed, if only in moderation.

The success of the Mediterranean diet is remarkable. Not only is it associated with longer life, it is also associated with lower levels of stress and less depression. People who eat the Mediterranean diet have lower levels of inflammatory disease, fewer heart attacks and lower blood pressure. It helps that this diet is great to eat. There are other diets but, for what it's worth, this is the one I believe the scientific data most supports. It is one I enjoy and so I like to recommend it.

All of this poses one problem for us in Ireland (and in northern Europe) – we don't live in the Mediterranean! We need our warm soul food. We like our hot potatoes and puddings. Our shared preference is for starch, and this is for a very good reason – these foods warm and comfort us during cold winters and dark evenings. This is why eating a more mindful diet isn't about moving everyone to the Mediterranean. In our whole new plan for living, this healthy eating is about introducing a more conscious balance. The old saying 'a little of what you fancy does you good' is still true. There is a great deal at stake in achieving this balanced dietary harmony. It's about a sustainable future for ourselves, for each other and for our environment.

The problem of comfort eating

Many of us eat in response to stress, rather than hunger. This kind of feeding behaviour is called 'comfort eating' or emotional overeating. Comfort eating is what happens when you go to the fridge without thinking, perhaps when you are frustrated or bored, and then eat random foods without much conscious thought. It is a lonely activity, and a response to some unmet emotional need that will never be satisfied by eating.

One dietary exercise could be helpful in making a whole new plan for living; it is to ask yourself whether you recognise an emotional pattern to your eating. Do you comfort eat? To help recognise comfort eating, ask yourself these questions:

* Do you eat alone and at irregular hours without thinking or feeling hungry?

* Do you eat directly out of the fridge or out of a packet?

* Do you tend to eat until you are full, and do you continue even though you are full?

* After you have eaten in this way, do you feel guilty, lonely, or even ashamed?

Comfort eating is an example of an 'alternative', dysfunctional behaviour. These behaviours are sometimes described as 'acting out'. 'Acting out' behaviours are often ways of injuring ourselves as an alternative to dealing with our unconscious difficulties and our deepest unmet needs. These behaviours are tangential responses to apparently inaccessible human challenges, such as our frustration and our anger, our loneliness, our emptiness and sadness, or in the worst of circumstances, our sense of self-loathing. Unfortunately, this acting out of our frustrations (in this case by our emotional overeating) leads to even more psychological upset and so the cycle of distressed behaviours goes on and on. Continuing to eat in an emotional way means continuing to eat long after any hunger has been satisfied. A feeling of morbid self-reproach is inevitable after the eating bout, so after the feeding is finished, we still find the original problems are left unaddressed.

Emotional overeating is not an easy problem to solve, but in our whole new plan for living we will find new ways forward. We will become more aware of the times and places when our life is out of balance, when our behaviours change, and we will know when and how to seek help if we need to.

Healthy eating plans are effective in addressing this problem because they acknowledge our *thinking* patterns as well as our need to change our *eating* patterns, thus making both thinking and eating more balanced, and making our eating a conscious mindful reality, not an unconscious mindless injury. Combined with the right motivation and help, a good eating plan will make all the difference. There is nothing fantastically novel or revolutionary involved. Recovery from emotional eating includes learning about yourself and your personal stresses, and begins by asking yourself what your triggers are for your dysfunctional eating behaviours. It grows through seeking help from professionals where needed and talking to someone trusted whenever you can. Making a whole new plan for eating well is not the same as telling yourself to pull yourself together. It begins with greater compassion for yourself and for your personal triggers. Bringing these into your consciousness will improve your recognition of other issues such as sadness, loneliness or boredom. By breaking the behaviour pattern caused by these unaddressed issues, the other ones that habitually make you overeat become clear. Once you recognise these feelings, you are one step closer to dealing with them.

Common emotional triggers for comfort eating:

- Loneliness
- Anxiety
- Shame
- Regret
- Anger
- Guilt
- Self-disgust

Keeping a diary

Keeping a diary can be a helpful way to learn more about your thoughts and behaviours. I like to include diary-making as part of a whole new plan for living. In attempting to overcome any dysfunctional behaviour or negative mood, a diary helps to monitor progress. For example, in emotional overeating a diary can help by setting goals and targets for more regular mealtimes and more balanced eating, and your diary helps you to recognise when things are moving in the right direction. And it is this success that encourages you to continue to monitor your progress. Making your results more tangible is one way of rewarding your better efforts and sustaining them. The diary-keeping method I recommend involves making a diary on a three-point scale. This is a very simple method.

This simple scale goes from +3 to –3 like this: +3, +2, +1, 0, –1, –2, –3. By letting each of these numbers reflect a subjective meaning for any behaviour problem, a longitudinal record will come into being. In the case of maintaining balanced eating, +3 is top performance, +2 is very good, +1 is good, zero is OK, –1 is poor, –2 is very poor and –3 is the pits! If we stick to our emotional overeating example, on a day when you've resisted an urge to comfort eat, note down your balanced meals for that day and at the end give yourself the +3 score. Then on a 'bad' day when you've given into the urge, note down why and choose which minus score to give yourself. Over time, a pattern will emerge.

Keeping a diary like this isn't about rewriting Tolstoy's *War and Peace*. It is simply a means of rating your success around the issue that you're challenged with and watching the pattern of your progress as you implement your whole new plan.

Learning more about your triggers and your progress through your diary can help you to identify what works and what doesn't, to understand what you enjoy and what you don't. It's a useful way to acknowledge your feelings to yourself and then plan for change. As with any great endeavour, it is important to measure your progress and then to gather the support you need around you.

That's why comfort eating is such a good example of a problem ripe for behaviour change. When tackling comfort eating, it's essential to resist the need to give in to your guilt or to allow self-reproach. It's more worthwhile, more compassionate and more successful to live within more achievable and more balanced goals. Commonly, when people fail to make progress with a behavioural problem it is because they began by setting their goals much too high. The resulting disappointment leads rapidly to a return to the old destructive behaviours. That's why people give up too early. It is better to lower the targets you have set for yourself and so increase your sense of achievement. Learn what works for you in small steps and then learn how to keep it working with regular rewards.

It's often been said that we do not eat to live but instead live to eat. In emotional overeating the story is rarely this simple. For one thing, blame is very common, and this is of no use. Remember that comfort eating is not limited by satiety or scarcity. Food use is not simply a matter of free will, and so, like many of our unhelpful behaviours, it is often sustained by our less conscious needs, and these are not readily visible to us. The discovery that much of what we do and say, much of what we think and believe, is in reality driven by factors outside of our conscious choice is one of the most therapeutic discoveries of our adult life. This compassionate insight is a provider of great relief and another valuable tool in the great task of making a whole new plan for living.

Food behaviours are a common example of behaviours prompted by our deeply unconscious drives. But there are many other 'acting out' behaviours besides comfort eating and these may be more relevant to you, but the principles are the same. It is no use telling someone that comfort-eating behaviour is their fault. Our whole new plan relies on a more refreshing and balanced approach to such difficulties. If our collective response to these unconscious behaviours becomes more compassionate, then our individual therapeutic paths to recovery will become more effective.

Sleep[xi]

It is said that Margaret Thatcher, former UK prime minister, was very dismissive of others' need for sleep. Allegedly she told her cabinet colleagues that 'sleep is for wimps', which goes to show how wrong she was about the importance of sleep to a healthy life. The average human spends a third of their lifetime asleep – and any behaviour that occupies this much of our lives must be a significant one.

Sleep is our most restorative daily experience – it gives the body and the brain time to get some essential chemical repair work done. So, when our sleep deteriorates, we must do something about it.

Sleep science reached a new level of recognition in 2017, when the Nobel Prize for Medicine was awarded to a group of 'sleep scientists' whose research helped to unlock the mystery of sleep. These scientists discovered the existence of genes they called 'clock genes', and their intrinsic relationship to the physiology of wellbeing. Clock genes are molecules governing the physical processes which depend on healthy sleep patterns. Good sleep enables their restorative functions and this sustains us.

Poor sleep has a major negative bearing on our health, and that is why doctors will frequently ask you, 'How do you sleep?' Sleep loss is a characteristic of clinical depression; likewise, our impulse control, work performance, mood and judgement all deteriorate when we are sleep deprived. When sleep is persistently lost, we can become very distressed and fall into a vicious cycle of insomnia and mental anguish; even minor degrees of insomnia can make some of us utterly miserable.

Sleep deprivation hinders all wakeful human performance. This is as true for truck drivers, shift workers and new parents as it is for doctors and politicians. It's foolish to think that some of us are immune to the harmful effects of sleep loss. Worldwide, sleep disorders cause thousands of road deaths every year.[xii]

The average adult needs between seven and eight hours of sleeps every night, but individuals vary regarding their absolute requirement. Young adults need more sleep than older adults, and some older adults need more sleep than others of the same age. The exact amount of sleep we need is an individual thing.

Distress and inflammation are the commonest causes of sleep deprivation. They're also its deadliest consequences. Any personal crisis – a bereavement, a relationship breakdown, a loss of employment, an emotional trauma, a physical injury – can disturb our sleep. If stress persists, then the sleep disturbance will persist. As the stress resolves, so too should the sleep disturbance. Unfortunately, when stress persists, the insomnia and resulting inflammation become enduring, and when our sleep loss is enduring, we are in peril.

There are many reasons for persistent sleep loss; they include common changes in the natural life cycle, and extend to include many serious illnesses. For example, many women going through the menopause experience enduring sleep difficulty. Shift workers and those who work at night have difficulty overcoming the body's natural rhythm. Sleep disturbance is associated with many general health problems and some commonly prescribed medications, such as systemic steroids used in the treatment of arthritis and other chronic inflammatory conditions. In all these circumstances, the best way to manage the sleep problem is to manage the underlying problem. The point is to prioritise our sleep and to seek an intervention directed towards the cause of its loss.

This is why in our whole new plan for living we will start by taking more time to wind down at night. We will shut off our screens and be quiet for a time before settling down. Going to bed at a regular time each night will also be helpful. A comfortable, supportive bed is important. Sleeping is easier in a darkened room and at a slightly cooler temperature than our living room. We all sleep better in a room that is devoted to better sleep.

Our daytime is the best preparation for our nighttime. Sleep is negatively affected by caffeine and alcohol use, as well as by nicotine. Drunken sleep is characteristically fitful, and so within two hours of sleep onset, any person that has consumed a large amount of alcohol will be awake again. This broken sleep is not just about an increased need to go to the toilet. It's because alcohol interferes with the healthy sleep cycle which moves early sleep from non-dream sleep to dream sleep (REM), and on again. This pattern of non-dream to dream sleep is a crucial sequence necessary for healthy restful sleep and it is always interrupted by alcohol.

One of the best decisions we could make as part of Step Two of our whole new plan is to give our sleep the priority it deserves and in doing so to make the changes that better sleep requires. Our sleep is precious, so it's worth trying to do it well.

Ten things we could do to improve our sleep:

1. Set an alarm in the evening to signal time to go to bed.
2. Avoid evening snoozing on the couch or mindlessly surfing the channels on the television.
3. Never bring work into the bedroom.
4. Turn down the backlight on your electronic devices (mobile phone, tablet, game console, the whole lot!) and switch them off thirty minutes before bedtime.
5. Avoid caffeinated drinks after 6 p.m.
6. Take exercise earlier in the day.
7. Avoid eating carbohydrates late at night.
8. Make a comfortable bed. Make it when you get up and you will look forward to it when you lie down.
9. Use blackout blinds to keep your bedroom dark.
10. Keep your bedroom cool.

Changing our sleep behaviours is challenging, but improving our sleep will be a very rewarding part of our whole new plan for living. If you haven't been getting good sleep for a very long while, don't try to resolve this problem all in one go. Put some small steps in place. It's enough for now to improve your sleep bit by bit.

Operation sleep restoration

Begin by making your bedroom a haven by banishing all associations with work from it. Move any filing cabinets, bills or work-related items that you currently keep in your bedroom and put them elsewhere. By doing so you will transform this place from one where you sleep only fitfully to one where sleep is your prolonged treasure. Start going to bed ten minutes earlier each night and do this for six nights in a row. At the end of the week you will potentially have had an hour's more sleep than you had the previous week. Each night as you go to bed, lower the lighting in the room. Maybe brush your teeth earlier to avoid the bright lights and the startling intensity of your bathroom, or install a dimmer switch there – many of us have bathrooms that are lit up more brightly than our towns. When it's time for sleep we need to get that clear message to our brains to say that this is 'sleep time'. Then, when you're ready, lie down. Try to be restful. If you can be mindful, now is a good time. If you pray, now is a good time to do that, but whatever you do to be quiet, do it now. Take your time to be at peace. Close your eyes and get yourself in a comfortable position, remembering that a good proportion of sleep's value is gained simply through restful reclining with your eyes fully closed. Do not count sheep and do not worry about going to sleep; instead just soothe yourself. Train your mind and body to be contented just to be quiet. Restful sleep is precious time and you're giving it to yourself in order to heal and to recover at the end of the day. It's a valuable gift to yourself, so try to avoid anticipation of the next day. Instead think of resting, for now. Thoughts like 'OMG, I have to be up early for a busy day tomorrow, so I have to fall asleep NOW!' will invariably lead to more insomnia. Instead let your sleep come as it may; just wait and take time to remind yourself of this truth before you go to sleep: you have done enough for today. Let tomorrow take care of itself and hopefully all will be well.

Exercise

Exercise[xiii] is an essential part of any strategy for healthy living, so in Step Two of our whole new plan we will renew a healthy respect for the value of exercise.

Exercise is certainly one of the greatest ways of reducing stress and mitigating our distress. I am repeatedly asked these two questions about it:

* Which exercise is the best – swimming, tai chi, going to the gym?

* How much exercise should I get?

My answers are very simple. The best exercise for you is the exercise you enjoy most. That is the one you can sustain most easily, as you will want to do it. The value of exercise comes from sustaining it, and by taking Step Two we are deciding to do the exercise that works for us. If you're a walker, then walk. If you like to swim, then swim. If you dance, then dance. It's a question of continuing to do the exercise that mobilises you and pleases you. So long as you get your heart racing, even just a little, then the exercise you do will be a good one.

Most forms of exercise are good for us. As with every judgement about our health, it comes back to balance. My reading of the data suggests that running is particularly effective for depression and anxiety. There is even some evidence that running can help you to live a much longer life, maybe even add years to your life span. But what if you're not a runner? Perhaps you are a swimmer or a weightlifter. Lifting weights can lift your mood as well. Swimming can soothe your anxiety. Swimming in a pool is good, but I have many patients who speak enthusiastically of the benefits of swimming in the sea (although this is not practical for everyone). One of my most anxious patients once said to me, 'You just can't worry while you swim. At least when I swim my mind is free from anxiety.'

There are people who feel excluded from the benefits of vigorous exercise, however. Only one fifth of adults over the age of thirty play a team sport and levels of participation fall dramatically by the age of fifty years.[xiv] Many people with a physical infirmity just can't do vigorous movement. Some exercises work for some people, but not for others. Like so many aspects of our whole new plan for living, the selection of your exercise is something very personal to you. It's not something anyone should prescribe, so I won't be telling you what to do. In Step Two of our whole new plan for living you have to write your exercise regimen in for yourself.

An exercise plan can be adapted for those who are disabled and for those in pain; in a similar way our new plan for living needs to be adapted around each of our individual challenges and difficulties. Even if access to your exercise is limited, let's think of ways to get through each difficulty. The benefits of exercise are worth extending to every one of us. The point is this: if we can, we need to exercise throughout life, and so we need to continue with our exercise plan for healthy living by doing things that are effective, sustainable, enjoyable, and compatible with who we are.

So, what about the second question, how much

exercise should we get? My answer is to take a little bit more exercise today than we did yesterday. If you walked yesterday, then walk a little more today. If you ran, then run a little more today. Each day, take the opportunity to increase your exercise, just a little. Choose to take the stairs. Get off the bus one stop early and decide to walk the remainder of your way. Find ways to extend your exercise by just a little bit more. Do it today. Enjoy it and keep doing it every day.

To sum up, these are the three key takeaways about exercise in Step Two of our whole new plan:

1. Make exercise a priority.

2. Do the exercise you enjoy.

3. Do a little more of it each day.

Reducing inflammation

Inflammation is the body's natural response to stress or injury. It's a chemical process that occurs throughout the whole body and the brain when we are stressed. The most serious stresses are not rare events, they are common, and they include problems at home and at work. Difficulties like losing a job or a breakdown in a relationship or even moving to a new house can cause great personal stress and inflammation. We will discuss the management of these in later sections of our new plan. For now, it's enough to understand that stress and inflammation involve the mobilisation of a variety of chemical messengers known as hormones or cytokines. These are part of our natural repair kit, and this process works by restoring our injured parts. In acute situations, inflammation is therefore a healthy and necessary phenomenon.

Unfortunately, chronic inflammation is like chronic distress. It is not good for us. Prolonged inflammation is toxic for the whole mind and body. The evidence is that chronic inflammation maintains an angry state that damages the very parts it was intended to repair. Recovery, like any healing, happens when this angry inflamed state settles down. Unfortunately, continuing distress results in even more widespread and more prolonged inflammation. Being in a permanent stressed state risks continued damage to the brain and body.

The inflamed experience in the mind and body is not limited to illnesses we traditionally regard as inflammatory, such as arthritis or diabetes. Chronic inflammatory states are sustained in mental health difficulties, such as depression,[xv] anxiety disorder and dementia. This understanding of chronic inflammation is underscored by our recognition of the 'wholeness' of our being – the lack of division between the brain and the body. Like viruses, inflammatory responses will go wherever they like. So, how should we prepare? What do we do to reduce inflammation? We apply all the aspects of Step Two from our whole new plan for living.

This means making positive plans for the everyday practical parts of our lives: diet, sleep and exercise – in short, our new healthy lifestyle. These actions may appear obvious, but they are essential actions if we are to make Step Two of our whole new plan for living as effective as it can be.

Now you have taken Step Two, it's time to proceed to the next step of your whole new plan for living.

Finding Ways to Greater Emotional Wellbeing

By now we have taken our first two steps and so we have arrived at Step Three of our whole new plan for living – increasing awareness of our actions for better emotional wellbeing. It's time to consider living in a more mindful way, that is to say living in the present, and non-judgementally. Many people struggle with mindfulness and in particular with aspects of meditation and relaxation.[xvi] In our whole new plan for living, we will embrace these things but not obsess about them. In this step, we will focus on four mindful actions and ensure these become the next parts of our whole new plan for living. These actions will build upon the changes we have already made in Steps One and Two. If you look closely you will see that Step Three also follows naturally from the eight dimensions of health and the five ways to wellness (see pages 5 and 9).

Four practical ways to improve our everyday (emotional) wellbeing are:

1. Being more compassionate (self-compassion)
2. Lightening the load
3. Letting things go
4. Becoming less judgemental

Self-compassion

All of us make mistakes, and yet we must carry on. Experience teaches us some valuable lessons, but the compassionate know that experience can be a very harsh teacher. Without self-compassion it will be hard to sustain a new way of living. Compassion for ourselves means developing an internal source of kindness. This creates the ability to soothe ourselves, to forgive our humanity and to comfort our being. This self-compassion is a good thing. It is like having a loving voice, always within us and always available to us, as a reliable calming aid, a source of warmth helping us to reduce our anxiety and ensuring that we get back on the road to recovery.

It's been said that 'bad things can happen to good people', but in reality, bad things can happen to anyone and at any time. The compassionate know this is true, but the ability to be compassionate takes its greatest battering when our mental health breaks down. Without self-compassion, this mental distress can exhaust even the most courageous person, and when this exhaustion persists it risks the ultimate loss of self-love, which is despair. Depression is made worse by a loss of self-love. Guilt thrives upon a negative background, and self-reproach is amplified by a lowered mood. The result may be a complete mental breakdown such as that seen with an episode of clinical depression. The technical definition[xvii] for this is 'a pervasive and persistent low mood that is accompanied by low self-esteem and by a loss of interest or pleasure in normally enjoyable activities … Major depressive disorder is a disabling condition that adversely affects a person's family, work or school life, sleeping and eating habits, and general health.' Depression becomes a darkening space, one in which the sustaining belief in the value of life may be in real danger. Mental health disorders (and most especially depression) account for a very large majority of suicides and suicide attempts; estimates vary between 60 per cent and 98 per cent of all suicides.[xviii]

Restoration of self-love is an essential part of recovery and of Step Three of our whole new plan for living. It's a source of new growth and it will bring with it refreshing new insights. One of these is the discovery that none of us is a hero and none of us is the absolute master of our fate. This awareness brings with it an even greater source of relief. The compassionate know the reality, that our future is not entirely in our hands. There may be times when we need to reach out for help from others to gather more resources for recovery. Seeking that help is too often delayed, but the recovered know the value of genuine help and this becomes part of their new plan.

In our whole new plan we will restore our self-compassion and this will serve to increase our balance, acting on the one hand to increase our appreciation of the value of our lives, while on the other hand accepting the transience of our experience. Great burdens of shame, guilt and frustration lose their power in the face of such understanding. When we strive, it will be for our happiness and for the happiness of those we love. As we learn to live, we will help each other and be uplifted by the most sustaining of emotions: kindness, especially towards ourselves. Compassionate self-kindness is not narcissism. It is a renewable energy source and a personal affirmation that is as essential to the continuity of our lives as the next breath we take.

Lightening the load: balancing work, rest and play

The stress levels of ordinary life have increased. Many people have been striving far too much while achieving far too little for our efforts. Constantly struggling to meet these increasing demands, from ourselves and others, is exhausting and unsustainable. The demands we put on ourselves include our desire for more security, greater perfection, more recognition, greater order and greater control. Sooner or later we will discover that complete satisfaction of our unconscious needs is not possible. Without this discovery, many of us just give up. In our whole new plan for living, it doesn't have to be this way. In Step Three, we will learn to lighten this load.

Healthy living is balanced. It includes as much rest as activity. In the workplace, it involves collaboration and teamwork, working with others rather than against them. Step Three values human joys and celebrates laughter. In our whole new plan, there will be fewer days without at least one good laugh. Ask yourself, 'When did I last really laugh?' If the answer is 'a very long time ago', then you need to make changes fast. You need a whole new plan for living now. Laughter is a huge part of our whole new plan. According to the Dalai Lama, laughing is actually 'the best form of exercise'. Step Three of our whole new plan involves making greater room for relaxation, rest and more LAUGHTER. By balancing work, rest and play (especially with some humour), we will restore our personal momentum. In this way our new plan for living is more likely to be sustained and our emotional needs are more likely to be nurtured.

Lightening the load is a strategic action as well as a human necessity. We need to make things easier so that we can carry on. If achieving all our goals required heroic stamina, we would wear out very quickly and would achieve very little in time. To find more healthy forms of emotional contentment, we need to balance our expectations of ourselves and mix them with more relaxation and more joy. Finding this balance will be difficult for many of us, especially those with an unconscious need for greater control, but as part of Step Three of our whole new plan for living, we need to remember to lower the bar of our expectations and so increase our chances of more sustained success. Our goal of better health will be achieved by greater engagement with this emotional part of the plan. Small acts of kindness mixed with more laughter will sustain us on the road to wellness far more effectively than giant personal leaps that are abandoned too soon. So, in Step Three we won't be trying to change the world in one go; we will plan for change, but we will increase our appreciation of it, little by little.

We can be healthier and happier when we lighten the emotional load on ourselves and so reduce the burdens on each other. This way forward in our whole new plan is a more practical form of mindfulness, and it is kind. It means greater sharing, more collaboration and more humour. Personal control is all very well, but the success of Step Three of our whole new plan for living depends upon our ability to lighten the load on ourselves and on each other.

Letting things go

The next part of Step Three, learning to let things go, is crucial to our everyday emotional wellbeing. It is a counterintuitive approach to stress management, since our modern, competitive world places so much emphasis on the very opposite – tenacity (not letting go). Some people in our distressed world recommend winning at all costs, while in reality winning is not all it's cracked up to be. Letting things go is wiser: it shows kindness to others and to ourselves. It is not necessary to win every battle, to gain the upper hand in every conflict, to score with every shot. The advocates for relentless tenacity create an impossible expectation and maybe even a dangerous one. On the other hand, the relief from letting things go is a genuinely compassionate route to our recovery and a source of much greater wellness in the real world. Paradoxically, letting things go is one of the most constructive things we can do in our whole new plan for living.

Some of us will find this more difficult than others

– it is not easy to let emotional things go, to shrug off slights and injuries, and to accept defeats without bitterness or regret, but it's no use returning to our daily battles with an even greater sense of injury. Hurts and offences can stick to some of us just like yellow 'post-its'. A once-wounded self is more easily wounded again. Step Three of our whole new plan for living is about finding a healthier, emotional way to give ground. It's a mistake to live our lives as though playing a tug of war, existing by pulling harder and harder, and giving not an inch to anyone. A healthier life is not lived by perennially saying 'no' to others, and so there are some things that we should just let go. Our emotional health would be better for some losses. Better emotional health must be more elastic, and so with Step Three we will bounce back.

Think about how exhausting it is to never let go – to hold out against every immovable fact of life and to contest every adverse force. Living a life defined by conflict is undesirable, unlovable and ultimately unsustainable. Instead, with Step Three of our whole new plan we will discover that it is not necessary to win every battle or to put every opponent to the sword. In conflict, as in life, timing is everything. Sometimes, the harder we pull, the sooner we tire. No amount of psychological effort resolves a tug-of-war mentality. Perennial combat means defeat for most of us, most of the time. So, before you start to do battle over any perceived slight, or to fight for any emotional agenda, ask yourself, 'Is this the ditch I want to die in?' If the answer is 'yes', remember that your opponent may be equally determined, and then if you persist you must be prepared for a bitter feud and potentially a bitter end. But if the answer is 'no', then this could be your time to acquire the power of letting things go. That's the power that Step Three can give you.

Let's be clear: letting go is not the same as giving in to wrongs or putting up with contemptible things. Our whole new plan for living is not just an excuse for accepting defeat, for resignation, for giving up. Letting things go is not a denial of our difficulties, and we cannot simply forget our problems and hope that they will no longer worry us. To put it simply, letting things go is not the same as 'moving on'. Step Three of our whole new plan points us towards a better emotional way to live, a mindful way. Our problems will continue to have power over us until we learn to diffuse their emotional effect on us. To do this we need to be strategic and mindful. Letting things go is about taking strategic actions while shedding our emotional distress, expanding our ability to continue more hopefully, to live and to love more fully. Often by giving ground, we become more patient than we were before and so much larger than our difficulties. It's a paradox, but there are times when giving way actually increases our chances of getting our way. In this way, Step Three helps us to move closer to other opportunities, closer to new solutions and hopefully closer to more joyful ones. Letting emotions go can liberate us from the visceral pain of our difficulties and free us to engage with new possibilities previously unfelt and unseen. Step Three is the ultimate anti-inflammatory strategy. Through it, we will see a better way to focus on the challenges we face and to embrace opportunities we may never have known before.

Becoming less judgemental

The pain of illness and of mental distress does not exist in a vacuum, it is amplified by our memories and by our judgements. In Step Three of our whole new plan for living we need a new mindful approach to this problem of emotional judgement. There is no good time to judge or to be judged. Negative judgement creates a hostile atmosphere that is toxic to recovery. Our response to those in difficulty is too frequently negative. Those who are ill, overweight or depressed tell me that they feel, firstly, labelled and then disabled by adverse judgement. The effect is only to increase their emotional burden. Consequently, the struggle to live well becomes even more difficult for those who have enough difficulties to begin with. In my experience, such negative judgement adds greatly to the inflammation of illness and so to its distress.

Negative judgement is almost always destructive. I

see it as a form of stigma. This judgement is not the same as discernment (which is wise), it is adverse judgement (which is critical) and it increases the pain of those who already blame themselves. Many people struggle to protect themselves from these critics, since the criticism of others increases the injury of their own critic, the unconscious judge, the one that resides within them. This is why mental health stigma has an evil twin – self-stigma, a critic more akin to shame and self-blame.

Becoming less judgemental will not be easy, but in Step Three we will seek to improve our emotional health and to make this change. None of us gets this right all the time. We can all rush in, just as I did on one occasion in my clinic, listening to one of my patients as he shared with me the story of his guilt and shame.

He was a married man with a history of depression and when I saw him, he was blaming himself for his illness and for the effect he believed it was having on his family.

'What should I tell my partner?' he said. 'I feel so guilty. She has had to put up with so much. I feel she blames me, and anyway I blame myself for my illness and for my lack of progress, my failure to recover. I can't expect her to put up with this for very much longer. I am a burden to her. She can't be expected to have limitless patience with me.'

His sense of shame was not confined to this

relationship with his partner. His guilt was profound, persistent and pervasive. He was experiencing an episode of deep depression.

'And what should I tell my employer?' he continued. 'They must have guessed something is wrong with me. Surely my depression is all my fault. Of course, I blame myself. Who else is there to blame?'

I listened before I responded. I wanted to counter each of his anxieties, to soothe each self-laceration, but then, inevitably, I rushed in and revealed my own point of view.

'Would we be talking like this ... if your difficulty wasn't defined as a "mental" problem?'

My patient paused, and looked at me as if to say, *What are you talking about?*

So I continued.

'What I mean is this: would you be as critical of yourself if we were talking about a physical illness, would you be judging yourself so harshly if we were talking about cancer rather than depression?'

My patient responded without hesitation.

'But Doctor, I would rather I had cancer. I would prefer to have cancer any day.'

There was nothing I could say. All I could do was listen. How could I explain what experience has taught me – that depression is more treatable than most cancers, that recovery is always possible, even probable, from most mental health problems?

We remained silent. Sometimes, no answer is possible. An adverse judgement would not have been helpful. A hopeful one would not have been credible.

This session with my patient was, as every therapeutic meeting should be, a 'listening conversation'. Every appointment should provide the potential for recovery. Seen in this way, his was just another revelation, a moment in what we call 'therapy'. But in this example I was the one who learned. Sometimes answers are for another time. It's the same for all of us. In making Step Three of our whole new plan for living we are progressing as one along a winding road to recovery, journeying together, becoming less judgemental. For sure this means more listening, and sometimes it's important just to stay there and listen, to share the painful space and, if possible, to sit with it, mindfully, non-judgementally, kindly, and hopefully until another time.

Being less judgemental is not about having a shorter list of dos and don'ts. Sometimes it means tearing up such lists and hopefully waiting for recovery to start again. That's why non-judgementalism is so important in our whole new plan for living. In Step Three we need to remember some things about our emotional mental health. Being mindful means being kind, lightening the load and being less judgemental.

Knowing this will give us time to persevere with a whole new approach to living. Being less judgemental helps us to breathe, to carry on and, ultimately, to live.

Step Four

Maintaining Health and Wellness in Difficult Times

We need to maintain our health and wellness, even at difficult times. In these situations, our whole new plan will help us to get through. In Step Four we gather our resources and learn to apply them in a more balanced way. We will need all our courage for the toughest experiences of life, but at those times we will need more than bravery, more than preparedness. After all, these are the times of our greatest losses, such as the loss of our work, the loss of our health, and especially the loss of those we love. In Step Four we will look at the practical application of all we have learned so far and consider how our plan could help us in practical ways at the most difficult times in our lives. We need to talk specifically about the tragedy of suicide. In this chapter we will focus on some common challenges in three key areas of everyday life.

1. Work

2. Relationship breakdown

3. Coping with death

Understanding stress at work

Work is an important element of a healthy life. Occupational health is one of the eight dimensions of our health, and so through work we achieve many of the five ways to wellness; we connect with each other, we keep active, we take notice, we keep learning and we give. Work gives us one of our most tangible opportunities to meet these physical, social and psychological needs.

It was Abraham Maslow[xix] who first ranked these agendas to create what he called a 'hierarchy of needs' (see diagram on page 77). For Maslow this pyramid represented the layered nature of our human priorities and of our motivations throughout life. Unfortunately, work can also be an experience that is unrewarding, and even dangerous for many people. In Step Four of our whole new plan we learn to address the challenges of work to maximise its benefits for us in terms of our whole new plan for living.

Maslow's hierarchy of needs

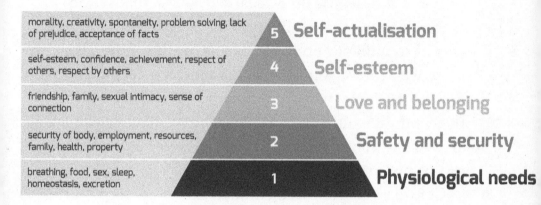

morality, creativity, spontaneity, problem solving, lack of prejudice, acceptance of facts	5	Self-actualisation
self-esteem, confidence, achievement, respect of others, respect by others	4	Self-esteem
friendship, family, sexual intimacy, sense of connection	3	Love and belonging
security of body, employment, resources, family, health, property	2	Safety and security
breathing, food, sex, sleep, homeostasis, excretion	1	Physiological needs

Maslow's hierarchy is a useful way of considering why we work and what work means for us. It's time to consider this for ourselves. At the ground level of his pyramid Maslow places our physiological necessities. These include our most basic bodily needs such as those for food, water and rest. Maslow described these as 'deficit' needs. In reality most of us work because we must, and so work is the way we meet our deficit needs. We work to pay the bills and to feed ourselves and to care for those we care about. But our deficits also include other needs for safety, love, belonging and self-esteem. Not all of our employments meet these deficits, and so for many people these basic needs go unmet at work.

Deficit needs are low down the pyramid. They exist in contrast to what Maslow calls the ultimate need for 'self-actualisation'. This is his term for the fulfilment of our whole human capacity. In our whole new plan, we could see this goal as representing the total fulfilment of our wellness. Maslow regarded 'self-actualisation' as much more than fulfilling our deficits. Work can help us to fulfil our potential, but as Maslow notes, the more we achieve some goals, the more we seek them. For some people, work can become a treadmill which they find difficult to get off. Once again, better health at work is about greater balance between it and the rest of our lives.

Considering our occupational health in terms of Maslow's hierarchy helps us to see how important work can be to us and how devastating unemployment can be. Work impacts our lives at every level of the hierarchy. Firstly, work is a way of meeting our basic physiological needs; secondly, it plays a major role in meeting our psychological ones. We are motivated to work as much by our need for sustenance as by our need for security, belonging and self-esteem. Without work it is very difficult to fill these deficits and difficult to achieve anything close to 'self-actualisation'. That is why the unemployed and those who do not work can be disadvantaged in so many ways. Work gives the employed the opportunity to fulfil their potential capacity, and because of this, loss of employment can be a very great blow.

Work can also be unhelpful in other ways. Many people have no option but to work in jobs they recognise as having no added value for them (other than to pay their bills). Work-related stress may be unavoidable, but the stress of work should be at most episodic and transient. Periods of increased stress may be recurring (as in an office at the end of the financial year), seasonal (as in retail at times of increasing seasonal demand) or intermittent and contextual (from issues related to hiring some people or letting others go). In each of these circumstances stress-related mental health problems are common responses to the increased pressures at work. The most prevalent of these stress reactions are anxiety, depression and substance misuse. At their most extreme, work-related stress problems can lead to mental breakdown or even suicide.

The understanding of work-related stress has changed since Professor Sir Michael Marmot[xx] began his research into the social determinants of health back in the 1970s and 1980s. He began by examining the occurrence of cardiac deaths in staff working in the British civil service at Whitehall in London. Back then it was generally believed that the frequency of heart attacks among senior civil servants was related to the weight of the responsibility borne by them. To everyone's surprise, Professor Marmot discovered this was not the case. He found two broad categories of work-related stress contributed to premature employee death: i) lack of support at work, and ii) lack of control of the working experience. These two dynamics (support and control) act independently of the other known causes of cardiac disease such as smoking, poor diet, high cholesterol and lack of exercise. Increasing volumes of work are associated with greater stress, but reduced 'control' (lack of autonomy) is also a toxic stress-related factor. Distress at work may rise with increased levels of responsibility and rising levels of burden, but a loss of the sense of support is a more important contributor to work-stress related injury.

The stress caused by an increasing workload is obvious, but these stresses can be mitigated by greater support and control. We have differing limits, but like everything else in life, our workload needs to be balanced with other aspects of our lives. Issues relating to support and control are often hidden sources of distress in the workplace. As workers, we benefit from more control and greater support for the issues that we give priority to. In Step Four of our whole new plan for living we will take the time to consider why we work, and understand our stress. The aim is to make work a sustainable part of our lives, not the unsustainable whole of it.

One way to reduce our distress levels at work would be to promote greater synergy in our place of employment, by harmonising the values of the employee and the employer. Without this synergy in the workplace, levels of employee distress inevitably increase.

To illustrate what I mean by synergy in the workplace, let's consider the distress experienced in forms of employment with a high level of 'vocational' commitment, such as education or healthcare. In these settings, respect, rewards and responsibilities of the worker are all finely juxtaposed. Once a teacher or a healthcare worker concludes that their work is no longer respected, appreciated or valued, their stress levels rise. If this continues, they begin to feel alienated, and begin to suffer through lack of support. When alienation grows in vocational settings it can lead to misery. Actually, the same is true in many workplace settings, from manufacturing to the service sector. Whenever an employee feels alienated from their work and unsupported, the result is poor productivity and increasing anxiety and distress. When this distress results in impaired mental health, it is damaging for both employee and employer, and in a broader sense, for both the industry and the worker's community.

So, how can we respond to these challenges of workload support and control to reduce our stress at work? This is as much a question for employers as it is for employees. A practical example of work-related stress in the everyday is the challenge of childcare. Some employers are supportive of their employees' needs in this regard, but others tend not to be. Suppose an employee is a parent: for this worker, access to childcare becomes a big agenda, and without support at work it may not be possible for them to continue working. This is a source of daily stress for many parent-employees, especially those engaged in low-wage and on-demand work. The supportive employer knows the benefit of providing access to good childcare. Greater support for childcare reduces the employee's stress and increases their engagement with their work. The unsupportive employer leaves the employee unaided and this stress is to the detriment of their health and their productivity.

Lack of control is also a significant source of work-related stress. Some employers expect their workers to sort all practical difficulties out for themselves, and if they do offer support, they make it so conditional that the employee has very little control over their work. This control problem has increased in the new post-COVID-19 work environment, where new forms of home/work–life balance have emerged. To paraphrase Dr Colman Noctor,[xxi] for many employees the issue of work–life balance is not a matter of 'working at home', but rather 'parenting at work'. Reduced control and autonomy adds to the stress felt by the employee, making it more difficult for them to resolve conflicting demands either at home or work. The resulting loss of control over work–life balance is a source of continued distress.

Wise employers understand the interdependence of the employer and the employee. The sustained motivation and commitment of each employee is perhaps the greatest asset of any service industry. Human beings are not machines, and even if they were, machines need maintenance and they also need down time. More enlightened employers have come to realise that the mental health of their workers is their most precious capital and so maintaining this is vital for the success of their business.

So, in Step Four of our whole new plan for living we will manage the stress in our workplace. We will begin to work in the interest of our health and wellbeing. By incorporating the following actions (each reflective of Steps One, Two and Three) and putting them into our whole new plan for living, we will have a better work experience and better mental health, even in the most stressful of work environments.

Take issues step by step

It's a mistake to look for global or comprehensive answers to stress-related work problems. A wise colleague of mine once told me, 'Never manage stress by examining the big picture. Stick to the small picture and let the big picture take care of itself.' Stress management at work or at home is best done in small steps, each taken one at a time.

Acknowledge stress

Get your rest. Remember what we learned in Step

Two: excessive tiredness, irritability and exhaustion are all associated with diminished performance and a loss of interest in the work itself. Acknowledge these things to yourself. By recognising that you could be burning out, you can help yourself in the interests of your mental health.

Look after your health

Remember Steps One, Two and Three. Take twenty minutes' vigorous exercise, at least three times a week. Try going for a run at lunchtime. Reduce the amount of caffeine and nicotine in your diet and this will improve your sleep. Getting better sleep – by going to bed an hour earlier and rising an hour earlier – will transform your sleep pattern and give you a feeling of more restful preparedness. Put structure into your day by giving it a beginning, a middle and an end. Keep a diary of your progress. Reward yourself for your successes. Be aware of your dietary habits – eating more regularly and in smaller amounts will make you feel more energetic and less bloated. Remember that postponing or skipping your meals at work is a bad idea. The combination of hunger and tiredness at work contributes to irritability, conflict and poor judgement.

Practise a mindful attitude

Remember Step Three. No matter what happens at work, try to keep your sense of humour. Join others in a conversation. If you find this difficult, try listening more. You don't have to be the loudest or the funniest person in the room – just try to communicate pleasantly. If you find that your mind is set against your employer, or one of your colleagues, ask yourself some emotionally intelligent questions, such as 'Is this conflict worth pursuing?' After all, it may be ruining the environment in which you are spending the bulk of your daylight hours. On reflection, you may find your conflict is not that important. Regaining command of your mental strength (by stepping back) is a more mindful approach. The politics and pressures of the workplace will not go away, but we must learn to manage them more effectively. It used to be said that rule number one for the employee was never to fall out with the boss. In today's work environment, the first rule is never to lose respect for your mental health. Step Four of our whole new plan is about helping each of us to manage our stress at work. Taking this much care of our mental health could be the best career move we ever made.

Managing conflict at work

Sometimes work stress arises from matters of human conflict, so how can we deal with these conflicts without damaging our health? Remember, you cannot avoid conflicts in work or in life. What matters is that you should never seek them.

A mindful approach to work means remaining aware of yourself. Self-acceptance is a great strength. Make a list of your stresses and acknowledge them. Then list your reactions and identify which of them is destructive. Avoid the temptation to enter rows with your colleagues. Sometimes, we engage in aggressive or defensive behaviours in unconscious ways – this is a form of 'acting out'. Rather than acting out, we could manage our distress more effectively by taking smaller, more hopeful steps, paying attention to little things and remaining positive as we go along, bit by bit – in other words, by being kinder to ourselves. Each of us will have our own individual ways of doing this, whether it is by keeping a picture of those you love on your desk or keeping in touch with the office sports league. Whatever you choose, learn to refocus your attention on more rewarding concerns.

Remember, we spend about a third of our day at work, so there is bound to be some conflict. Step Four is about applying what we have learned in Steps One, Two and Three, by renewing a commitment to our wellness (Step One), taking better care of our physical health (Step Two) and remaining mindful of our emotional wellbeing (Step Three). When we are in the thick of stresses and confrontations, we see them as very important, even as matters of life or death. Step Four is an opportunity to recall our self-worth, to be compassionate to ourselves and to remain non-judgemental even in the face of difficulty. Our conflicts are rarely as significant as we think, and difficulties at work are more transient than we realise. Don't wait for others to change. Longing for our colleagues or our circumstances to improve is pointless. It's a mistake to see work as all good or all bad, and even stressful work can be a part of healthy living. In Step Four of our whole new plan we will manage our conflicts at work the same way that we manage everything else: by starting with ourselves and making changes to our own emotions and behaviour.

Surviving stress, including conflicts at work, means remembering to take care of the body and the mind. It is about doing this for yourself as much as possible and whenever you can. Remember, taking these steps for your wellbeing will deliver results in good time. Take that early night for rest, enjoy that pastime you have let go for too long. Call that friend for a chat. Get some sleep, some exercise and some laughter into your life once again. Remember that tiredness, irritability and exhaustion will damage all your relationships. When you are stressed at work, look to your joys, not to your wounds. Patience with yourself will increase your performance both at work and at home. It's better to wait before sending that 'final' email, and don't rush to dispatch that angry text message. Keep your balance. Patience and self-care are key to survival in any conflict.

Negative automatic thoughts (NATs)

Let's consider one specific example of a difficulty at work (and then try to apply this to any difficult situation you might be having in your work). The disappointment of not getting a new job brings up many painful feelings. Step Four is an opportunity to consider such an experience in a new, more balanced way. What does the decision not to appoint you say about your potential employer? Suppose it says as much about them as it does about you. Over the years, I have interviewed and been interviewed many times, and more often than not I have not succeeded in getting the job I was going for. From experience, I have come to understand one thing: the merits of every candidate for any position are important, but they have only a partial bearing on an employer's decision to hire a particular person for the job.

Whether consciously or unconsciously, the employer appoints the person they think will best fulfil their needs. It's as simple as that. This successful candidate is not necessarily the person with the brightest future, the widest range of skills or even the best qualifications. Employer perception is the largest factor in employer decision-making. This explains candidate selection more than anything else, and it means that excellent candidates with great qualifications and potentially great futures encounter disappointment every day. The task of getting that job may be more about your perceived 'fit' than about your 'fitness'. This may not be fair or right, but in my experience it's the case.

It follows that to draw a negative personal conclusion from a failed job interview is a big mistake. Failure to get a job feels like a negative reflection on the unsuccessful candidate, but when a 'failed' candidate generalises from this disappointing experience, they make a logical error, becoming needlessly downcast. This reaction, unless it can be reframed, will continue and lead to further failures. There is a saying that goes, 'nothing succeeds like success'; the same is true for perceived failure.

Following a failed interview, the candidate may think, 'I didn't get this job, so I am never going to get any other job in this industry ... that job was the one that was going to change my life – my failure is catastrophic for my future!' But it's a mistake to draw a subjective personal significance from such a disappointment. Negative conclusions like these are destructive, and even though they seem justified, in reality they are completely illogical. Such negative thinking promotes the development of what American psychiatrist Aaron T. Beck called 'negative automatic thoughts' (NATs).[xxii] These are thoughts that can extend from one 'failure' to another and seep into every aspect of our lives and our self-esteem. An experience of failure does not have to become a measure of our self-worth. It's a setback, not a judgement on who you are. You can fail at anything and still not be a failure.

This negative thinking can affect any part of our life: our living, our working and our loving. In Step Four of our whole new plan for living we will adapt to the difficulties we face in everyday life by recognising our NATs and reframing them.

According to Beck (the father of cognitive behavioural therapy), these errors of thinking arise from three areas of our concern: for ourselves, our world and our future. Other examples of generalised NATs might be:

'I know that I am always going to be found out.'

'I am weak.'

'I cannot ever be happy unless ...'

Even minor setbacks can perpetuate a sense of failure by further validating our deepest NATs, at the expense of other, more positive experiences and hopeful data about ourselves. When our everyday disappointments (whether at work or at home) resonate emotionally with our negative core beliefs about ourselves, our world and our future, the effect can be long-lasting. And although these core beliefs may have been suppressed in the unconscious for a long time, they can easily be rekindled or reignited by some further disappointments we may experience. In this way, our negative core beliefs amplify negative views about the self, the world and the future. This is known as the cognitive triad, as described by Beck, and it is a negative thinking paradigm commonly found in people who are depressed. Examples of this kind of negative thinking include:

'I can never be happy unless I am successful.'

'The world will always reject the things I do.'

'My future is always going to be bleak.'

Set against this negative background, each further setback amplifies some negative core belief, and as each is felt more deeply, the cognition becomes more depressing.

In Step Four we will acknowledge our NATs. Our disappointments may be objectively real, but our reactions to them may be more damaging. We can continue by acknowledging our setbacks and learning to respond in a whole new way. Subjective pain may be based on objective experience (for example when we don't get that appointment or when we lose someone we love), and there is no point in denying this pain. We may lose in this way again and again. These losses cannot be rationalised and these traumas cannot be ignored. Nevertheless, the evidence is that even in these circumstances, amplifying our experience with more negative thinking is unhelpful. Disappointment is part of life. All of us have hopes and dreams, and yet most of our plans will never materialise. Only a narcissist expects to have their own way all the time. A purely individualistic model of the world, one that is built upon the fulfilment of our separate ambitions in a population of more than seven billion people, would be a nightmare.

Think for a moment of a future in which each of us got our own way, all the time. Think of a world where everyone had complete determination over what happened in their lives. It's an impossible prospect. Sometimes not getting what we want is a necessity, even though it is disappointing. In Step Four of our whole new plan for living, we will learn to respond more hopefully to our disappointments. The loss is bad enough, but the sense of disappointment may be even more damaging. We will identify our NATs and remember that our response to life's stress can be triumphant, despite our failures.

Disclosing a history of mental disorder to your employer

One in four of us will have a mental health problem in our lifetime; 75 per cent of adults with a mental health problem had this before the age of twenty-five.[xxiii] From this data, it follows that many people in the workforce must have a history of mental health disorder. When we talk about 'disclosure' to our employer, we mean deliberately informing them about our mental health history. This kind of disclosure is a major step.

The dilemma of whether or not to disclose increases the anxiety of those returning to work or applying for a new job after an episode of mental health difficulty.

It persists and remains a burden for those with a past history of a mental health issue. People ask themselves many questions when returning to work after an illness: Should I tell my employer and my colleagues? What is the safest thing for me to do? What will happen to me or to my career if I do choose to disclose? What's the legal position?

There is good reason to be concerned about this issue. Many people believe their employment and career will be damaged if their employer learns about their mental health difficulty. They worry about negative reactions from their employer and colleagues. The scale of these experiences is indicative of the continuing level of stigma faced every day by employees with a history of mental health difficulties.

Part of the problem is misinformation. Many people are unaware of their rights and responsibilities. This information gap is understandable given the sizeable body of legislation and the case law that covers the issue, but thankfully, there are several helpful guides for employees and employers. So, here are the facts.

Mental health issues are classified as disabilities in employment legislation, and so, rightly, many people are protected by this legislation. These laws are also in place to develop a mentally healthy work environment by encouraging employers to take appropriate measures to support their workforce, including those with a difficulty.

There are two main groups of equality laws

pertaining to employment: the Employment Equality Acts (1998–2011) and the Equal Status Acts (2000–2011). These are based on European legislation, and so there are similar laws throughout the rest of the EU. In addition, there is legislation relating to health and safety at work in the Safety, Health and Welfare at Work Act (2005). There is also European legislation in relation to data protection under what is known as the General Data Protection Regulation (2016).[xxiv]

To discriminate against an employee means treating one person less favourably in the workplace than another person in a similar situation because of their disability. The law recognises nine grounds for discrimination and one of these is disability,[xxv] including mental health difficulty. It follows that a mentally healthy work environment is one in which everything reasonably possible is done to reduce the negative impact of work stress. Discrimination should not be part of the work environment. An employer is expected to make 'reasonable accommodation' for someone with a mental health difficulty, ensuring that 'appropriate measures' are in place so that someone with such a problem can have access to their employment, to participation or advancement in employment, and to training. However, these 'appropriate measures' must not place an undue burden on the employing organisation.

Mental health awareness is an essential part of

modern life. Everyone benefits from creating a mentally healthy work environment. In this way, the skills and contributions of those with a history of mental health problems are not 'lost' to an employer or to society. Instead, the creation of a mentally healthy culture at work improves staff loyalty and increases productivity.

It may surprise some people that there is no obligation on any citizen to disclose their mental health issues to their employer. Neither is an employer entitled to ask whether an employee has ever had a mental health issue. Simply put, people with a history of mental health problems have the same rights to privacy as anyone else – there may be no need to disclose the illness to anyone. It could often be the case that a particular mental health problem or difficulty has nothing to do with an individual's work or their ability to perform a particular set of tasks safely.

So how do we negotiate this dilemma? What does Step Four of our whole new plan for living say to us about it? Ultimately, it is for each employee to decide whether to disclose or not. This decision is about the culture of the workplace and the integrity of the employing organisation. A decision to disclose is influenced by issues related to the individual disability, but also by the stability of the work environment.

Any just legal framework must attempt to find a balance between common sense and fairness. Health and safety regulations may be invoked by employers in certain circumstances such as where medications may interfere with the use of machinery, so it may be necessary for both employees and employers to understand what's involved. Both parties have rights, and both have responsibilities. Ideally, both the employee and the employer will contribute to the building of a mentally healthy working environment. No one gains in a culture of 'don't ask, don't tell'; everyone gains in a culture that is mentally well.

Burnout at work

In 1981, psychologist Christina Maslach and her colleagues at UC Berkeley defined the consequences of severe occupational stress.[xxvi] She proposed the first valid and reliable scale for the measurement of the phenomenon we now call 'burnout'. This problem has three distressing features: emotional exhaustion, diminishing personal achievement and depersonalisation. This last feature is the loss of belief in the value of our occupation. It manifests as an unprecedented or uncharacteristic cynicism in the employee, causing them to distance themselves from the demands of their job.

Burnout is common. It has been recognised in workers in almost every stressful occupation – teachers, nurses, doctors, social workers, firefighters, lorry drivers and even in members of the clergy. It is a common consequence of persistent work stress in the context of rising expectations and diminishing resources. Burnout is not a disease. It is closer to an occupational injury. In our whole new plan for living, the task of looking after ourselves means acknowledging our risk of burnout. Step Four means seeking a proper remedy for those who are currently experiencing this debilitating problem.

The discussion about the causes and remedies of burnout concentrates on the negative impact of increasing stress and diminishing resources. This is consistent with the data from the Whitehall Studies of Sir Michael Marmot and his colleagues mentioned on page 79. This stress relates to the balance between the 'load' placed on an employee and the support given to the workforce. Wise employers understand the need to balance the stress placed on employees by providing better support resources for their workforce. The concept of lifelong employment with a single employer has changed, and most workers can expect to train and retrain many times over the course of their working lives. Still, workers deserve a realistic prospect of support in their employment.

When we look at the causes of burnout in this way, the demand for more support becomes reasonable. In Step Four of our whole new plan for living, consideration of burnout also directs us to do more for ourselves, by actively managing our work–life balance, our time, our diet and our exercise. In other words, the issue of burnout calls us to be strategic and make changes in our lives.

The most dangerous feature of burnout is depersonalisation. Burnt-out social workers, doctors, firefighters and teachers all have one thing in common: they no longer care about their work, and this depersonalisation is very distressing for them. The solution is not straightforward – better time management and more hours spent in the gym will not remedy this fundamental break with the meaning of their occupation. In Step Four the remedy for burnout lies in rediscovering the value of our relationships and increased collaboration. We should start, however, by examining our relationships with ourselves. Guilt and self-reproach should have little place in our hearts; we need to be able to soothe ourselves, especially when our work has exposed us to great trauma. We may find this difficult to do, but it is essential.

Compassion (especially self-compassion) is fundamental for us as it enables us to continue working post-burnout – we all can tire in the workplace and we cannot always depend on the support of others. Some people get stuck regretting the passing of a former time in their work environment, but this is a mistake. Today's workplace is changing and it is a hostile place for some of its labourers, but it can also be a wonderful and supportive place. We need to remain hopeful.

The evidence is that worker burnout is mitigated by three things: better work–life balance, better personal care and more collaboration or teamwork. Support in the workplace works best when it is enhanced by growing cultural engagement, more enlightened leadership and greater teamwork. In Step Four of our whole new plan we look towards a more mindful workplace. Burnout occurs less where the value of a healthy workforce is understood by management: where there is support for staff in distress and where all staff are enabled and encouraged to take better care of themselves.

Relationship breakdown

The breakdown of a relationship is one of the most common causes of stress and distress. Studies in Europe and the USA suggest that up to 40 per cent of first marriages end in divorce.[xxvii] Three-quarters of these people will re-marry, but unfortunately many of these second marriages will also end in the divorce courts.

The consequences for the health and wellbeing of separating couples are substantial. Instances of distress, ill health and premature death all increase after a breakup. Compared to married adults, separated or divorced people have increased volumes of illness from all causes, and their mortality rate is increased by 23 per cent after divorce.[xxviii] The reasons for this morbidity and mortality are a complex mix of all the known psychological, social and biological stresses that can act adversely upon our health and wellness.

The volume of distress is even greater when we include people going through breakups of non-marital relationships, partnerships and close friendships. Relationship breakdown is one of the most stressful experiences any of us can go through. It is up there with death of a spouse or a stint in jail, and it is complicated by all the difficulties associated with poor health and wellbeing, including financial upheaval, loss of social network, parenting issues, and potential loss of identity. After a breakup many people ask themselves this question, 'Who am I without my partner?'

Despite this scale of difficulty, most people recover from breakup trauma – and in time, they find a new way to live. For some, this is a better way. Recovery from relationship breakdown has all the characteristic features of any successful recovery. This includes the ability to restore connectedness, to continue to hope, to discover personal identity and to live a personally meaningful life. There is, however, a substantial minority of people (between 10 and 15 per cent) who continue to struggle long after a divorce. The risks are greatest for those with poor health before the breakup.

Alcohol abuse is an important factor in many marriage breakdowns, both in predicting marriage breakdown and negatively influencing recovery. According to American psychiatrist George Vaillant, the question is one of 'the chicken and the egg'[xxix] – which comes first? It's a similar story for other mental health difficulties and breakups. One fifth of the population has a history of anxiety/depressive disorder prior to divorce, and six out of ten of these will experience a depressive reaction after a breakup.

Those who survive difficult times to live long and happy lives have two characteristics: they continue to value love, warmth and relationships, and they maintain positive ways of thinking. So, in Step Four of our whole new plan for living we will shift towards these more positive emotions and remember that staying mentally well is key to our resilient ability, especially at times of great difficulty.

Coping with death

Death is a normal part of life. To some extent, the fear of death is ever-present in our minds (either consciously or subconsciously). Death has no hierarchy. These things are obvious, but they are largely unsaid. Death is intimate and personal, unique and universal: unique because we are unique, universal because we will all die, and so in life we will grieve for our friends, for our families, and for everything else that we love: our pets, our homes, our dreams and our future. We grieve for what we have lost and for what we might have had, because we love and because we lose.

Even as we deny all this, it's true, but greater awareness of the reality of death does not have to be morbid or melancholy. Awareness of the transience of our lives is mindful and it can be liberating.

Grief

With death there is always grief and many other emotions besides this obvious sadness, such as anger, regret or even relief. The complexity of our bereaved feelings is one reason why there is no normal way to grieve. We will all be bereaved at some stage, so none of us can avoid this pain forever. Grief is the price we pay for loving and for being loved. Feelings of denial, anger, bargaining, depression and acceptance are common after the death of a loved one, but these should not be seen as 'stages' in a prescribed or phased sense.[xxx] Grief is not a sequence. It is a personal and universal human experience.

The loss of a child is the hardest grief for any adult to bear. Bereavement through suicide or violent crime is also extremely painful. We cannot simply 'accept' these losses and 'move on'. We cannot minimise our grief or other people's.

Grieving is made more difficult by bitterness and disputes within families. A death that is complicated by blame, guilt or shame – such as the death of an abusive parent – will be more difficult to bear, not less. Cynics of the grieving process have said that, 'Wherever there is a death, there is a family, and wherever there is a family there is a row.' It's true that families can be blighted by infighting at funerals, by the settling of old scores and by the division of the mourners themselves into the worthy and the unworthy. Only those living suffer when this happens. Thomas Lynch,[xxxi] the undertaker and poet, famously said that 'the dead don't care'. If this is true, it contrasts sharply with the plight of the grieving.

We speak of grief as 'complicated' or 'stuck' when it becomes burdened by additional feelings of hopelessness, despair or even suicidality. Complicated grief is slower to ease. Those stuck in grief are less able to consider a future life that is lived without their loved one. The good news is that even complicated grief can be mitigated by kindness and time. Most people appreciate genuine support from their friends and family. Others find the sanctuary of private time invaluable. Some cling on to those they love; others prefer to stand alone. Everyone is different, and so there is no right way to grieve. Although the bereaved never forget, even the most complicated bereavement may be followed by the rediscovery of a whole new plan for living.

So, what should we do when we are bereaved? What could our whole new plan for living say about our grief? Are there practical steps we can take? The answer is yes. Step Four of our whole new plan is about the practical application of our skills for living, of restoring balance and being at peace. So here are some things we could do. You will know which of these best suits your circumstance, but here goes. This is what Step Four says to me.

If you have some social support, take it. If you have faith, try to keep it. If religious practice is part of your life, then bereavement is a time to deepen it, if you can. If not, then don't blame yourself for your loss of faith. Most of all, be kind to yourself. And if you are on the side, comforting the bereaved, just listen. Don't impose your beliefs.

Bereavement continues even as grief diminishes. Anticipate and prepare for difficult anniversaries – the first Christmas, the birthdays, and the empty chair at the dinner table. Take time to think ahead. Make plans for especially challenging times. Seek solace from trusted friends. Avoid illusory comforts like drugs and alcohol and try hard not to run away. Dismiss others who tell you there is a right way to grieve or that it's time to move on. Grieve your own way and feel free to do it when and while you need to. Always remember that things will get better – in time.

What about our own death?

Today, we speak less about death than previous generations. It's not easy to explain why this is so. Our tendency to sanitise death could be out of respect or consideration for the bereaved, but it could also be a form of denial. Notice how we refer instead to 'passing' or 'passing on', as though the words 'death' and 'dying' have become impolite. Death is the last taboo. We speak little of it and so we are less prepared for death. We acknowledge death happening to others 'tragically' rather than 'naturally' or 'inevitably'. That way we stay out of touch with the inevitability of our own death. Perhaps this is the way it is meant to be.

Every day, we are told that more of us are living longer, but people are dying no less frequently. We keep our potential death below the radar. Our remains seem less visible. Compared to our parents' and our grandparents' generations, we are less likely to keep a dead person in our house, or to wake them through the night before the funeral. Many people have never even seen a dead body, still fewer seen one that is laid out at a wake.

It would be good for us to acknowledge our mortality. We need to discuss our death and prepare for it. In Step Four of our whole new plan for living we will speak openly about it – but not in a morbid way. We need to express our preferences and make a will. Death in this modern era throws up many previously unthinkable issues – the management of our social media being just one of them. One of my patients highlighted this for me: 'After I pass on,' she said, 'who will manage my Facebook page?' It's an issue no one could have worried about until recently. When making a will we should consider how we would like our family to remember us at our death. An enduring power of attorney may be helpful for those of us with ongoing health problems. The concept of a 'living will' is also a good one. This is a declaration of our intentions in circumstances where we are alive but unable to discharge our wishes without support: for instance, we could be unconscious. Irish legislation has been passed to establish a Decision Support Service. When fully implemented, this legislation will have profound implications in these circumstances.

Greater acknowledgement of death would be good for us. A fear of dying is understandable, but being conscious of our death helps us to be more mindful about our lives. There are practical things we could do today about our death that would make a real difference at a later stage. We could start by talking about these things to those we love. This conversation does not have to be strange or awkward – our aim is to ensure that our wishes are respected and that nothing is left after our death that will cause unnecessary additional pain to those bereaved. Step Four of our whole new plan for living includes making a whole new plan for dying.

We can consider practical things. What, if anything, do you want done with your clothes and your belongings? One patient of mine arranged to have all her friends come to her house after her death and then each of them was invited to take a piece of clothing as a keepsake. Decide whether you want a service, religious or otherwise, to be held to mark your death. Prepare for things, if you have time. Buy a grave or give instruction regarding your cremation. Think of the content of any service and state whether you would like a eulogy. Think of those left behind and make sure that nothing you advise will add to another's pain.

Funeral services can be a great source of consolation to the bereaved. Remember, you won't be there, so it's even more important to think of others. Think of these things and make your personal preferences known while you still can. These death issues may seem trivial, and some of them may be, but they are also important. The point is that by considering these things now, you are doing your mental health a great service. Acknowledging our mortality and preparing for our death is good for our health.

Suicide

More than four hundred families in Ireland have lost someone by suicide in the past twelve months.[xxxii] Most of us have known at least one person – a friend, a colleague, a neighbour, a family member, someone in their child's school – who has died by suicide.

Nothing I am going to say here is intended to increase the pain of suicide[xxxiii] for those left behind. Talking about death by suicide in this context could help us do two essential things: to show respect for those who have died and to give support to those who have been left to grieve.

Suicide is best understood as a catastrophic

behaviour. It is not a mental illness. Throughout our history and in every society, women and men have killed themselves; some of them have done this without being mentally ill. That said, and this must be acknowledged, most people who take their lives are experiencing extreme mental distress or disorder at the time of death.

We no longer talk of people 'committing suicide'. The act of suicide is no longer thought of as a sin or as a criminal behaviour, so the reference to commission of suicide is not just outmoded, it is unkind. Severe mental illness is the most common cause of suicide. This death is equivalent to the heart attack that consumes a woman with untreated angina or a burst aneurysm that destroys a man with severe vascular disease. It is equivalent to these tragedies because like a heart attack or a burst aneurysm, death by suicide is most often the result of a disorder. It is a catastrophic end of a life in someone with a serious health problem; a sudden, unexpected and unforeseeable outcome of an acute mental health difficulty.

Many people consider suicide (or just not being here anymore) at some stage. Some people in distress find themselves in a 'space' where they begin thinking 'if I didn't wake up tomorrow, all this pain would be gone' – and so for a time (in their distress) they don't want to be here anymore. This may be hard to believe but it's true. There are different patterns of suicidal thinking and you don't have to be mentally ill to consider suicide. Thoughts of self-destruction can come to any of us, and not just at stressful moments in our life. These dangerously destructive thoughts may arrive as part of the strain of daily living or in the anguish of a tragic loss. Some think of suicide more compulsively, and with death-wish thoughts that are frightening to them. These thoughts are especially terrifying when they return repeatedly in a ruminative pattern despite every effort to put them out of the mind.

For a small minority of people, the idea of suicide comes as a relief. This situation is very dangerous. A suicidal logic can grow until it becomes compelling. Then the balance of a life may tilt quite suddenly, and if it does, a suicidal plan seems suddenly more reasonable, more justified, more a solution to seemingly insoluble problems than a catastrophe with devastating consequences for all. When this overwhelming rationale begins to surround a person, it can enable the act of self-destruction. Strangely, before this form of death, the suicidal person may seem sanguine, suddenly relaxed, relieved, and even happy in the sight of others. A person experiencing this mood is at their time of greatest jeopardy. Recollection of this incongruous mood adds to the bewilderment experienced by those left behind.

When talking about suicide to those bereaved in this way, I always try to steer away from answering the question 'why did it happen?', because the reality is that no one will ever know. Questions about who, what, when or where will come, but for now the bereaved need responses that are more compassionate, kinder and ultimately more useful. The question of why the suicide happened risks drawing us back to speculation and to blame.

And yet this is the question that keeps coming back, keeping people's grief raw. It is essentially a question about the unknown. The answer is that for some reason the dead felt their death was their best or only option. We cannot dismiss the act of suicide or try to rationalise it as healthy or reasonable, and it is a mistake to describe suicide as a choice – it's more complicated than that. At some point before they completed suicide, the person felt they had no other way forward and they could not see beyond that moment. In bereavement, we can only guess at their ultimate motives. Sometimes, in notes and last messages, the dead appear to ask us for forgiveness or understanding, but often they leave us only unanswered questions and more time to grieve.

Talking to children about suicide

Childhood is meant to be a happy time, a protected time, but for some children, especially those prematurely exposed to death as a result of a suicide in their family or community, childhood becomes a particularly challenging time.

When there is a death by suicide, we need to be able to talk to each other and to our children about what has happened. Sometimes, when we are in pain, we cannot find the right language to explain what we are feeling. We communicate only with our presence, by our gestures and by our willingness to listen and to reassure each other. Yet how should we speak to our children at these times? There are no easy answers to the questions posed by our children after such a death. Death by suicide occurs twice a day in Ireland. Each day adds a new dimension to this supremely painful conversation some people must have with their children. Thankfully, helpful guidance, based on a combination of experience, science and common sense, is available from a variety of responsible sources. For those affected, seeking that help is worthwhile and often essential.

I will try to summarise some key points on this topic. Just as there is no right way to grieve, there is no right way to speak of that grief to each other or to children. We can only do our best in these extremely difficult circumstances. One thing is certain and reassuring: talking about a death by suicide to a child does not cause a death by suicide. In fact, such a conversation may prevent it. So, how should we have this conversation with our children?

There are some first principles. Firstly, children have a right to know about death. They have a right to ask questions and a right to be heard. Secondly, adults have a duty to be as honest as possible, and to be appropriate when they talk to children about suicide. No matter how difficult you may find this (and it is difficult), it is essential that your child gets this information from you rather than from other, potentially ill-informed sources. Remember that children at differing stages of development have different levels of comprehension, depending upon their maturity. For example, pre-teens and teenagers are likely to have very different abilities to express or comprehend their loss. We need to take this individual variation into account.

It is worth preparing what we are going to say. After every death, a conversation such as this may happen at any time, and it is best to have given it some thought and some preparation. There is no harm in rehearsing what you are going to say when you talk about a suicide with your child.

The first thing is to look after yourself and your own feelings. The shock and suddenness of loss through suicide is stunning. It's best to remember that the causes of suicide are never straightforward, and no one has all the answers. In your grief and confusion, try to avoid others' gossip or speculation about the death. There is great value in a period of deep quiet before this conversation begins. Take your time. Give yourself space to cope emotionally. Whether the deceased is an adult or a child, the mix of emotions will be powerful. Give yourself latitude to cope with your own mixed feelings before you approach your child.

The next step is to care for your child. Remember, your adult grief does not exist in a vacuum. Your concern for yourself will likely be quickly followed by intense concern for your child. Your awareness of his or her grief is a good thing. As your child's welfare becomes a priority, be prepared for their different ways of handling their grief. Their sadness may be expressed in intense, short bursts. Between these times, they may not communicate, so be prepared to catch the moments when a conversation is possible.

Do your best to speak in a simple way. Avoid euphemisms. Stick to language that is easy to understand and be as honest as you can be. This includes sharing your shock and bewilderment, your anger and your sadness. Try also to acknowledge the validity of your child's feelings. Be ready to hear about their sadness, confusion, anger and lack of understanding. Listen to them. Sometimes, a child will simply say, 'I don't know what to think or say.' Acknowledge this too. Sometimes, it's hard for any of us to know what we feel or what we should feel. It is OK to be distressed. Do not reproach yourself or your child for the way that you both feel.

Next, it is best to acknowledge any rumours and

questions about the suicide. Try to put them into context and be particularly careful with social media in this regard. In time, the manner of death by suicide, its causes and its specific circumstances will be made clear. Soon these facts will diminish in importance and be replaced with a deeper truth: the realisation of the finality of the loss. Much more communication will be needed along the way.

It is important to recognise the dangerous and often unintended consequences of self-harm behaviours. Remain non-judgemental. Never preach or lecture, but emphasise the danger of risk-taking, especially around drugs, alcohol or firearms. Suicidal behaviour is a learned behaviour, though obviously it is not a learning model to be followed. Some children feel inclined to copy the behaviour of the deceased. This risk has been seen among siblings, cousins or schoolfriends, leading – albeit rarely – to groups of deaths known as 'cluster suicides'. It is important for adults to avoid alarm about 'clustering', while remaining vigilant at the same time. Once again, active listening and better communication is our best safeguard.

Children, like adults, struggle to understand the reasons for suicide. In the absence of any other explanation, young people are more likely to blame themselves for what has happened. Some children even feel that a parent who died by suicide could not have loved them enough. In both situations, it's important to hear this distress and then to try to reassure the child. As far as possible, nothing about the manner of a death should take away from the good of a life lived or diminish the love in that life for those who shared it.

Sometimes after a suicide, people stop talking about the deceased. As a result of this silence, those left behind, particularly the children, find themselves simultaneously bereaved of their loved one and prevented from grieving for them, without permission to give voice to their cherished memory. In time, talking with each other may make it possible to offer an alternative explanation, at first tentatively, that the deceased must have felt so confused or so terrible that they came to a dreadful conclusion – that no other solution existed except their own death. An opportunity to talk with a trusted adult on these lines can make all the difference.

It's important for adults to affirm that nothing in life should ever be so terrible or so devastating that suicide becomes the best option. With the appropriate help, a better option can become reality. Ultimately, we want to ensure that all our children have the confidence and freedom to reach out when they feel hopeless, so that they seek more help when they themselves feel depressed or despairing or in a crisis. Earlier intervention and more effective mental healthcare will only be accessed if we hear each other's needs and respond with effective support.

So, what more is there left to say about Step Four of our whole new plan for living – maintaining health and wellness in difficult times? Simply this: life is very hard and it's harder for some of us than we acknowledge. There are times when we all need help just to get us through. Remember that remaining well in these most difficult times is possible, and that these are the times when it is most important to take care of yourself, practise self-compassion and seek help.

Step Five

Recognising a Mentally Healthy Life

To some people, 'mental health' is just a catch-all term, referring to a group of capacities involving our thoughts, feelings and behaviours, but to others with a certain kind of experience, mental health is something more precious, something that needs to be nurtured. Some of us know how mental health can be lost and we also know how it can be found again. This is the understanding of mental health that matters in everyday life. And it's essential for the next step of our whole new plan for living.

The human experiences we associate with mental health are located in an intangible place we call 'the mind', and so we use the term 'mental health'. Our descriptions of difficulties in our mental health lack concrete definition. Psychiatrists like myself use 'diagnoses' to get around this problem. These mental health diagnoses are simply descriptive terms used to describe some of the most prevalent types of human distress that anyone can experience.

It follows that there is no test for mental health or for mental illness. This is one of the facts of mental health. The validity and reliability of all our mental health diagnoses depends upon the quality of the sufferer's description and upon the duration of their observation. Serious mental health difficulties, such as schizophrenia or bipolar mood disorder, may be apparent more objectively, since these problems may be witnessed and experienced in ways that are more obvious, more measurably described and therefore more easily identified over time.

The more common mental health difficulties, such as anxiety disorders, depressive disorders and addictions, are not as easy to classify, but the distress they cause is still evident to our friends, families and even ourselves. The incidence of these common mental health difficulties is rising in our society, at a great cost. Taken together, both serious and common mental health difficulties account for a very large proportion of the demand placed upon our health services.

Mental health problems are important because they are perhaps the largest source of human suffering and loss. Severe and enduring mental health difficulties shorten human life expectancy by between fifteen and twenty years.[xxxiv] Although this shocking statistic has been confirmed through years of research, it is rarely highlighted, and so this is the next fact of mental health that we must acknowledge. The life and death aspects of our mental health problems should make us more concerned about these difficulties, and they should increase the priority we give to our mental health – but they don't. I have no good explanation for this neglect, but in my experience, it is a fact. In Step Five of our whole new plan for living it's essential to acknowledge the facts of mental health in everyday life by accepting that we still have much to learn about the nature of our own mental health and wellness.

These are the things we need to know about our mental wellbeing. I like to call these 'the facts of our mental health'. I have mentioned some of these already.

The Facts of Mental Health

Since human beings are formed as one entity, there is no division between our brains and our bodies. This unity of the mind and the body is a physiological, biological and psychological truth. Restoring our

The facts of mental health:

- There is no test for mental illness
- Serious and enduring mental health problems shorten life expectancy (by 10 to 20 years)
- The mind and body are one
- There is no health without mental health
- Wellness transcends illness, it exists before it and can exist after it
- Naming the experience is the first step to recovery
- Anyone can have a mental breakdown. The experience is not rare and neither is recovery.

mental health in our whole new plan for living begins by recognising the eight dimensions of health, but this is not enough. We need to use these eight dimensions as foundations of our physical and mental wellbeing, and to do this using all the evidence that confirms the unity of our mental and physical health. So, this is the next fact of our mental health: 'there is no health without mental health'.

The next fact is similar, and it follows from the last. Since there is no division between the body and brain, the things that are detrimental to our bodily health are also detrimental to our mental wellbeing, and vice versa. That is why Step Two of our plan is so important and why stresses caused by poor diet, a sedentary lifestyle, obesity, overwork or underwork, cigarette smoking, alcohol and drug misuse are all associated with much poorer mental and reduced physical wellbeing.

When acute stress affects us, its impact is experienced in our mental and physical health. Our whole being responds to crises via its automatic biological 'fright, fight and flight' response. As a result, any substantial hazard in our life is met with an innate set of physical reflex responses. These are primitive whole-body and whole-brain processes. They are unconscious and very persistent.

When a great hazard comes along in everyday life, we automatically respond rapidly to defend ourselves and we naturally take fright. We become flushed. Our hearts beat faster and we prepare for a fight. Our hair stands up and, next, we sweat. This outpouring of the body's natural adrenalins and stress hormones instantly mobilises a special adrenalin-fuelled energy within us. Blood flows to our limbs and we prepare to run. This instinctive process, which has been the basis of our defence since prehistory, is also the basis of our modern-day panic, which can be triggered without any objective evidence of danger. The acute symptoms of our distress are experienced throughout our being, traversing every system from head to toe, escalating from alarming palpitations, to dread fears of our sudden death. No one who has experienced or witnessed a full-blown panic attack could be in any doubt that the brain and the body are one.

We have already agreed in Step Two to take some restorative actions – better diet, better sleep and increased physical exercise – and in Stage Three to take actions for our emotional wellbeing by becoming more mindful. Now we are at a new stage in our whole new plan for living. We must increase our chances of living well by integrating Steps One, Two and Three by seeing in their synergy the restoration of our everyday physical, emotional and mental wellbeing. In our whole new plan for living, there can be no divisions, and so from now on we will see the route to better health as a kind of three-legged stool, where the first leg is physical health, the second mental health, and the third lifestyle and behaviour.

Actions around these three elements will combine to make our strategic new plan effective, to reduce stress and to soothe our inflammation, and so to restore our health. By including these steps, we will go a long way towards improving our health in all three areas. This will help us to deal with the difficulties of life (Step Four) and prepares us for Step Five – the restoration of our mental health. Our whole new plan for living takes effect through these steps by helping us to adapt to stress and so to reduce the risks of further disease.

It's essential to understand the synthesis of these steps from a mental health point of view. None of these plans or steps involve large, dramatic or unmanageable changes. In every case the healthy answer to our distress is to achieve a new form of balance; in each case the route to this new healthy equilibrium is a gradual one. In making our whole new plan for living, we must avoid the rookie error of trying to do too much too soon, the mistake of biting off more than we can chew. At every turn in our plan we will achieve success because, by lowering each bar, we will be jumping over more fences. In our whole new plan for living we are aiming for sustained success, not a flash in the pan. Rebuilding a healthy, more balanced relationship with yourself and with others in a more sustained way will bring us together, recovering bit by bit, achieving better health as a whole and not in broken pieces.

Achieving a mentally healthy life

We go through life coping with difficulties that cause us stress, anxiety and worry, and our worries have increased as a result of the COVID-19 pandemic. Step Five of our plan is about achieving better mental health at any real time, so that we have greater opportunity to live well in everyday life, and do this despite our worries. A mentally healthy life can exist in ordinary reality, not just in some imaginary zone. We may see this mental health as being unachievable, but witness of recovery has taught me this: mentally healthy living can be achieved in the real world with all its difficulty.

The language of wellness – as expressed in the eight dimensions of health we discussed earlier in Step One (pages 21–33) – may be unfamiliar to many of us, so in order to make progress with our mental health we may need to translate this into something more practical, more personal and more meaningful. This process of translation is part of what we call therapy, and it is another reason for us to make a whole new plan for living. Without a conscious plan, without a useful translation of our distress, without tools for our wellbeing, many of us just carry on with our lives, coping with difficulties we cannot name, searching for a wellness we cannot describe.

Some people tell me they 'just don't get mental health; surely we just have to pull ourselves together?' Others talk to me about their difficulty understanding why other people 'suffer so much in their mind' and they wonder why 'some people behave the way they do'. Still others describe their own anxiety and panic in terms that they cannot explain. One patient of mine called this her 'nameless dread'. None of these problems with comprehension is the same, except that all of them illustrate how challenging it is to respond with clarity to seemingly intangible mental health difficulties.

Achieving a better understanding of our mental health in everyday life is essential. The crises in our mental and physical health can be so frightening and bewildering, especially at times when we are dealing with the unknown. But as Louis Pasteur once said, 'Chance favours the prepared mind', so with a whole new plan for living we will become more aware and more prepared for whatever life sends to us.

One of the most frequent questions I hear from people at the beginning of a mental health crisis is, 'What is happening to me?' It could be depression, an anxiety attack, an addiction or even a psychosis, but this bewilderment is typical of mental difficulty and is very distressing. It tells us something about the hidden nature of these forms of distress. Most people are surprised and unprepared for a mental crisis when it comes, but it does not have to be like this. With a little preparation we could be more ready and more understanding of ourselves and of others.

So, how can we achieve this awareness? Where do we find this translation of our difficulty and this authentic understanding of our way forward? At this stage, further steps may not be possible on our own, and it may be time to consider seeing a counsellor.

Counselling

People often ask me whether I think they should go to a counsellor. Recommending a specific counsellor is not an easy thing to do. So Step Five of our plan could be simply asking the question, 'Would therapy help me?' To help you answer this question for yourself, some simple clarifications may be helpful.

Choosing the right therapist for you

Any useful counselling relationship is a deeply personal one, and so one person's trusted relationship may not be another's. There are many different types of therapists, from addiction counsellors and psychologists, to psychiatrists. Each one offers a type of mental health service, but each does this in subtly different ways. Some still work alone, but most of us nowadays work in groups known as multidisciplinary teams. Key skills within these teams include psychology, psychiatry, mental health nursing, occupational therapy, social work and pharmacy (prescribing medication). This diversity is good, even though it is difficult for many people in distress to understand, and so for anyone who is considering getting counselling, it can be difficult to know where to start. My discipline is psychiatry. A psychiatrist is a medical doctor who specialises in the mind. Like every other member of the team, we work towards an individual's recovery, but a psychiatrist does this by bringing a medical point of view to the job of planning each individual's care.

Going back to Step Five, in practical terms, I always say that it's best to discuss the question of psychotherapy or counselling with someone you can trust – your GP, for example. This is a discussion you should have sooner rather than later – many people delay for years before getting this kind of help. So my advice is to talk to your GP as soon as you feel you are struggling.

So, what is it like to see a counsellor, whether a counselling therapist or a psychiatrist? As I have said, each of these professionals is different, but at the risk of generalising, there are some things we can say about every form of effective psychotherapy.

Firstly, psychotherapy should be a restorative experience, not a traumatic one. Ideally, it should be an anti-inflammatory experience, even though, as in any relationship, it will have its twists and turns. Understanding these ups and downs turns out to be a great source of recovery, since these difficulties may be reflections of inner conflicts that have not yet been identified or addressed. In therapy, it's important to use each of these difficulties for the benefit of recovery.

The most important person in any therapy and any therapeutic relationship is the patient, and so the benefits of therapy derive mostly from the quality of the relationship between the patient and the counsellor. When someone decides to see a therapist, they are embarking on a search for a special form of trusted relationship, one that is dedicated to their recovery. This clinical engagement needs to add more empathy, not more distress. I would not recommend anyone to persist with a counselling relationship which they perceive to be uncomfortable, destructive or unhelpful.

It should be something special and should grow in the context of 'a listening conversation'. Therapy is a listening conversation – we start by listening to each other and we make progress by hearing each other. Gently, and over time, a therapeutic relationship grows. Within this connection, we develop a mutual investment in a trusted dialogue. This is as it should be; after all, both of us want to get it right. We are all aiming for recovery even if there are times when only one of us believes that recovery is possible.

Although each kind of therapist may belong to a different discipline, they will have had years of training, learning the specific techniques of their form of therapy. In practice, instinct or common sense prevails, and this sense tells both the patient and the therapist where to start and when to finish. Inevitably, in therapy the parties to the conversation move in time beyond simple diagnostic interviewing, and then something more dynamic happens. Trust grows, and as this deepens, something else very significant also happens: the unconscious works.

To paraphrase Michael Balint, the great psychoanalyst of the therapeutic relationship, it is also important to remember that 'the doctor (the therapist) is the drug'.[xxxv] By this he meant that the person providing the counselling is like a drug, and so the practice really needs to be understood – and it is something that we really need to govern. We need to know as much as possible about therapy's risks and much more about its side-effects.

Understanding therapy

The classical Freudian therapist was supposed to function rather like a blank slate – a tabula rasa – onto which the patient's mind could be projected and analysed.[xxxvi] Through this projected mind the patient's 'transference' and the therapist's 'counter transference' are sources of understanding and ultimately of 'insight'. It is not my intention to critique this method, but a truly blank state of this kind probably doesn't exist. This classical picture helps me to remember that therapy depends on building a relationship of trust. As a therapist, it's always necessary to walk this professional line, to establish boundaries and to maintain propriety. It's essential to remain clinically 'appropriate' and balanced in order to remain helpful and therapeutic.

Therapy has come a long way since Freud, and now there are many other forms and other sorts of communication that can be therapeutic in the right setting. These include voluntary supports and twelve-step agencies of all kinds. Most doctors, whether they are general practitioners or psychiatric specialists, give advice and reassurance as well as medicines. These modes of dialogue are the most common forms of 'therapy' found in medical practice. We know very little about the science of their effectiveness, but we learn from our patients telling us what works for them. This therapy is part of our need for human connection and so it's mutual.

Many people seeking a counselling psychotherapist are looking for more than a reassuring human connection, and this could be what Step Five is all about for you. It's time to start asking this question about therapy for us.

It's important to recognise when advice and reassurance is not enough. Persisting with these may even be harmful. Apart from objective professional errors in medicine, other professional risks also exist from non-specific reassurance. In some therapeutic relationships there is even a potential for 'sham medicine'. This is the sort of psychotherapeutic treatment that exploits a growing dependency between the therapist and the patient. This is an absolute abuse, and when it arises it says as much about the unconscious needs of the clinician as those of the patient.

So, how do you know who is the best therapist for you? The best therapist is always someone who is available, affordable, likeable, accessible and most importantly trustworthy. The value of the therapist is not only a function of the method of therapy – it's about the human quality of the therapeutic relationship as well as the professional training and skill of the therapist. Therapy's value is in the connection. That's what works.

Cognitive behavioural therapy

The most popular form of modern psychotherapy is cognitive behavioural therapy (CBT). This type of therapy aims to help us learn new ways of perceiving ourselves, our world and our future. We discussed a little of this in Step Four when we mentioned how CBT can teach us to overcome depression by recognising our characteristic ways of thinking, by challenging our negative automatic thoughts (NATs), and by rejecting deeply held negative and destructive emotions. With this educational, learning, and conditioning approach, CBT teaches us not to be crushed by the bad stuff that happens in life. CBT can also help us to address long-held negative beliefs about ourselves, just as it teaches us to prepare for a better future.

When going through CBT we become more able to recognise the NATs that underlie our thoughts, our emotions and our actions. We learn to recover our health and to continue with life despite the NATs. We come to understand that we do not have to live at the mercy of our negative thinking.

But CBT is just one example of an effective psychotherapy. There are many other modern therapies that can also help us on the road to recovery.[xxxvii] In Step Five of our whole new plan for living we will reconsider therapy and be more open to seeking professional help and to considering some specific form of psychotherapy. Step Five says that now is a good time to find out what might work. Maybe CBT is one of the therapeutic paths that could help to manage your negative emotions or maybe other psychotherapy paths would suit you better.

In the end, therapy can teach us that our emotions are just that – they are brain events. They are no more and no less than thoughts or feelings – and as with our most negative thoughts, they are best left where they are. The mind is a personal, private and sometimes very painful place, but it's also a potentially wonderful, imaginative and hopeful place. Talking to someone about our mental health difficulties could be an important step in our whole new plan for living. We need to support more opportunities to consider this restorative therapeutic engagement in every way we can.

Modern therapy is effective because it helps us to regain mastery over our brain and restore us to a mindful life. A trusted counselling psychotherapy can help us to recover oversight of the whole of our health and so be well again.

The importance of listening

Over my years in mental healthcare, I have often been reminded of the importance of counselling and of listening help. Therapists[xxxviii] are trained to listen carefully, but this compassionate listening is not exclusive to those trained in psychotherapy. We can all listen to each other. We need to acknowledge what many people do. Women and men working in the health services listen every day to people talking about their lives and their deaths. Volunteers in organisations such as the Samaritans listen compassionately. People listen in families and in schools, in communities and throughout the whole of healthcare. The point is this – their listening is also therapeutic.

Without listening we will not hear, and so we will find it much more difficult to learn. When we listen, we begin to hear each other, and so we come together to solve our problems. This shared listening continues wherever there is a compassionate and therapeutic ear. We may struggle to know how best to respond to distress, but with Step Five of our whole new plan for living our struggle will be resolved. One thing is certain: the best therapy starts with listening.

Achieving wellness

This leads us to the next fact of mental health. Recovery is possible. It transcends disease. We will examine recovery in more detail later (pages 212–224) but this is a hopeful fact and an essential insight necessary for everyone in distress. Recovery involves this discovery: wellness exists before illness, and it can be restored after it. Any illness can interrupt our wellness or even co-exist with it, but illness does not proscribe wellness.

In Step One we learned that our health is not an absolute. Paradoxically, we can have a disease, or even several diseases, and still be well.

The wellness we seek is associated with a sense of continued personal energy. As the poet William Blake put it, 'energy is eternal delight'. This well of energy is the capacity to go on living and loving despite our pain, being sustained by greater hope, greater acceptance and more commitment to a healthy life. When we are ill and in search of this wellness, in order to recover, something therapeutic must happen to us. This 'something' is the beginning of any sustained recovery and it often emerges from some form of therapy or counselling. It is the ability to recognise and name our experience.

A more hopeful therapeutic reality begins with naming things as they are, and with this identification our priorities change and a new understanding arrives. Ultimately, we learn that there is no health without mental health. This is another fact of mental health.

Naming our mental health difficulty

My patients have demonstrated this insight with more authenticity than I can ever record. So now in Step Five I would like to share with you (with their permission) two separate examples of this experience of naming things, of acknowledging things, to illustrate the power of their understanding. One example comes from a woman who was explaining her recovery (after a breakdown) to me, and the second comes from a family I met after the tragic death of their father, a man who died by suicide. By juxtaposing these stories, I do not intend to suggest they are equivalent. There are no winners and no losers in mental health, but it is important to acknowledge that sometimes illness leads to a tragic outcome even while most people survive to achieve a new and potentially enlightening recovery.

To the first person I simply said, 'Tell me about your recovery. What part of therapy worked for you?'

'Nothing seemed to be working for a very long time,' she said, 'and then I began to see what was really happening to me and so, as I finally recognised what it was, things began to improve.'

'And what did you begin to recognise?' I asked.

'I realised that I had been having a mental breakdown,' she said, 'and once I could name it, things began to improve for me. My recovery began by my calling "it" what it was. Now I had a name for it and so I could accept it.'

It's worth reflecting on this for a moment. This woman's experience may seem naive – even unbelievable – but it's actually very real. Too many of us struggle to find a language to describe our mental health, our ill-health and our distress, until we are confronted by experiences we cannot understand and challenges we have no name for. We struggle with our 'nameless dread'. The naming of these things can be very demanding and also very frightening, but through therapy, acknowledgement can reduce our fear and this is another step towards recovery.

Every health issue has its own form of language and likewise mental health therapy involves learning a new form of communication, but this can be a route to recovery. The language of a health crisis is always alarming. Cancers spread (or metastasise). Infections can become septic or contagious. Aneurysms can burst. But in mental health difficulty we can 'break down'. In all my years I have not found a better way to describe this experience: a 'breakdown' is the greatest crisis of mental health.

It's not easy to acknowledge any of this, let alone to understand it, but in my experience of therapy I have found that speaking the language of mental health and wellness is helpful. Not everyone is prepared for this dialogue, but in Step Five of our whole new plan we're saying perhaps it's time to make a start now and to be open to it. These words are part of an acknowledgement that is the basis for recovery. Deep down, we know that mental distress is a reality. Now we must communicate with each other in therapy to learn that recovery can be our reality too. One day, mental breakdown could be our experience or at the very least the experience of someone very close to us. This is the next fact of mental health: we are all breakable. Any one of us – or any part of us – can break at any time.

The challenge of speaking about therapy and recovery in this way, of explaining it and trying to understand it, is even greater after a tragic death. This may be when the need for a therapeutic understanding and acceptance is at its greatest. That is why I will never forget one conversation I had with a family who had lost their father to suicide. In medical terms his last illness had been 'a severe depressive disorder with features of an acute psychosis on the background of a long-standing addiction (in remission)'. In human terms through his deep distress, he ended his life. How could anyone explain his death?

I met with his family soon after the death, as I always try to do. These types of meetings are among the most painful experiences in my professional life, but my difficulty is as nothing compared to the suffering experienced by the bereaved. The bereaved family asked the clearest questions, and listened carefully to the sincerity of my answers.

We sat together for a while until they started to speak.

'We have a question for you, Doctor.'

'Of course,' I said, 'please ask me anything and I will try to tell you what I can.'

'What killed our father?'

The directness of the question stunned me for a while and, as I recall, I paused for a long time searching for the right words. This therapeutic time hung around us all like a dead weight, and so in some ways my lack of coherence mirrored their own frustration. I was aware that none of my 'psychiatric' terms or medical language could adequately explain their terrible loss.

Instinctively I responded by abandoning the jargon.

'The truth is, I don't know why he died,' I said, 'and maybe none of us can ever know exactly why he ended his life. All I can say is this … that I knew your father very well; we talked about his depression, and over the years I saw his suffering and I came to the conclusion that his depression was like a "cancer" in his mind. In my view it is that "cancer of the mind" that killed him.'

They sat with me for a time, in silence at first, and then they began to weep. To my surprise, the eldest responded by saying:

'Yes, that makes sense, thank you for telling us. I understand what you're trying to say, and it's helpful to see it that way.'

They continued to weep together as they comforted each other.

Of course, no therapy, no words, are ever adequate

for all the challenges of health and ill-health, still less when it comes to the reality of death. My explanation may have been unsatisfactory on many levels but that is what I said, and it is what I truly believe. For this family at least that was enough. We may accept that we have a broken leg or even a broken heart, but accepting that our mental health (or the mental health of someone we love) has broken is still too much for many of us to do. Still, recovery in the aftermath of a loss starts with a recognition that any of us can break down. Identifying this truth of mental health enables us to work together towards individual and collective repair. Empathy starts with the realisation that next time it could be us.

Looking back now, it seems to me that my female patient put it very well when she told me about her therapeutic breakthrough:

'This breakdown of mine was a frightening experience but naming it has been a sort of liberation for me, and do you know why?'

'Tell me,' I said.

'Because by naming it, I rediscovered that I am a human being and I am also breakable. I can break. And I did break. Now I know that my illness was an experience that any woman or any man could have had. My distress was part of being human. It was part of being alive.'

'And so, are you well now?' I asked.

'Yes, thankfully,' she said. 'In fact, that's the point. Don't you see? My breakdown has changed me. Now my breakdown has become my breakthrough.'

After Step Five we need to look further for the way forward. We need to make this whole new plan for living our very own.

Step Six

Making This Plan Your Own

It's time to get personal. It's time to make our whole new plan our very own. We've made a good start by agreeing on a number of things in Steps One to Five, so now let's continue by considering these issues with greater confidence; let's do this every day. By making it personal, your plan will be more relevant and therefore more useful. You will become more able to look beyond yourself and be more prepared to consider many wider aspects of our shared health and our wellness.

Have no fear. We can still do this together. Making a whole new plan for living will continue to be a collaborative process, but along the way we will consider other related but critical issues together and hopefully will learn a great deal. Let's begin by agreeing to progress with our new personal plan and to do this with a greater recognition of our individualism. This means developing a new understanding of our personal concerns: who we are and who we want to be. In short, let's take this time to consider our identity. This step begins with the recognition and acknowledgement of ourselves. Let me start by explaining why this recognition is essential to the progress of our whole new plan for living.

The search for identity

An authentic new plan for our lives must include a genuine acknowledgement of who we are. This acknowledgement requires a fresh recognition of our rights, and ultimately a greater degree of acceptance of our personhood. In the clinical world of 'disability' (in which I have worked for so long) we have a mantra for this recognition of individual human rights. This is a standard we should apply to all our new life planning. This mantra says: 'Let there be nothing about me which is without me.'

Respect for our identity is a fundamental principle of our whole new plan. When it comes to planning your healthcare, it follows that you are the primary agent of any change; and you are also its principal beneficiary.

So, in Step Six of our whole new plan for living it's time to ask yourself this fundamental question: 'Who am I?'

Answering this question means acknowledging, perhaps for the first time, issues that are unique and personal to you. These personal agendas are the things that define each of us, and considering your identity is at first a private activity. You may have never considered some of these things before, or they may have been ever-present in your mind; it doesn't matter. Have no fear of making your enquiry – no harm will come from this exploration. In every life there comes a time when it is essential to ask these questions, and your reward will be a unique set of answers. Taken together, these insights will ensure that your whole new plan for living is right for you, ready to grow into something more relevant and authentic around you.

You will recall that before we started on Step One, I asked you to begin the process of making your whole new plan with just a few things: a hopeful heart, an open mind and a blank piece of paper (see pages 15–17). In guiding you to do this, I was setting the scene for this stage in our process. Now is the time to use those tools to put your identity down on this blank page. Even now, after coming this far, I can understand that you may be inclined to draw back – there may be a part of you that has always been sceptical of such personal introspection. But please let me assure you, it's going to be alright. Before you abandon the whole exercise, think on this: nothing will be achieved unless we can have trust. Trusting in yourself will allow you to trust in the whole process. After all, you are at the heart of this. Even though this phase of planning may be very unfamiliar to you, I promise you it will be worthwhile, so stick with it, and remember that some personal exploration is always necessary.

Surely minding your health and happiness is no less important than buying your first car or even making your will? Each of these prosaic tasks involves an exploratory process, and one that is guided by a structured method. So why not give the same due diligence to the understanding of your unique role in your own health and wellbeing? Every time you visit the doctor, you are asked to share something of your story and this narrative is stored as notes. This record-taking is made according to some long-established method. Why not continue making your whole new plan for living with a similar structured process? Making your own record in this way will at least put you in charge. You will own the data and own the process. If it is formed in this way, your whole new plan will be all yours forever, and from the very beginning.

So, get your piece of paper. Give it a heading. Put your name and the date on top of it and then pause. This is a new beginning. I want to help you to form a picture of who you are, where you're going, and how you're getting there. This structured process is about you and so it should not be rushed. Your whole new plan cannot, will not, continue without YOU, so remember, this could be the beginning of the most relevant part of your whole new plan.

Who am I?

There are no right answers and no negative marks in this exercise, but don't be surprised if you have to tear up many versions of yourself before you're happy with the result. Take your time. Start by making a fresh image of yourself. Draw a big circle on your blank page and then place yourself firmly in the middle of it. Ask yourself some personal questions. Start with 'Who am I?' and then 'What am I?', 'What is my life and what is in it?', 'What is my identity?' Put your answers down on paper. The authentic answers to these questions may elude you for a while but give it a try anyway. By answering these questions and visualising them, you're beginning to identify your most important unmet need – yourself.

1. Who am I? What am I?

2. What is my life? What is in it?

3. What is my identity?

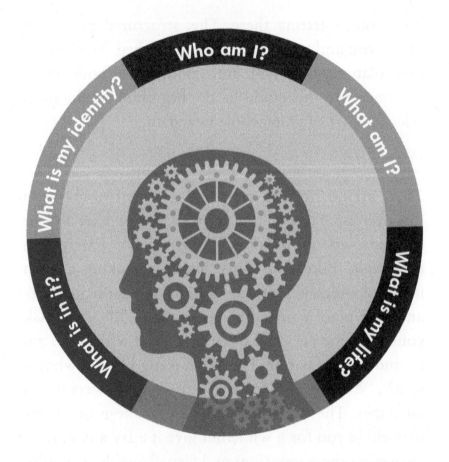

Identity is one of the key items described in the recovery acronym CHIME (CHIME signifies the features of recovery and these are connectedness, hope, identity meaning and empowerment). These questions about identity have no easy answer, yet they are essential if you are to recognise at least some of the personal issues most relevant to your health and wellbeing. It's essential that you continue your whole new plan for living by recognising yourself, knowing who and what you are.

Most people begin this task in Step Six by reducing their identity to absolute, easy-to-understand categories. By identifying ourselves in this way we begin to recognise, organise and understand ourselves as human beings – gender identity, race, sexual orientation, and so on.

After a while you will begin to see that these categories are not enough – human beings cannot be reduced in this way. The recognition of our identity is more than a psychological game of who's who. Surely there is more to us than a limited set of labels? We are diverse and so we must be able to look beyond. So, to describe a more authentic identity, most people try to extend these basic themes and add to them. By adding many more to the list we can fill out our description and make it real. Let's continue by adding as many descriptors as we can: Rich or poor? Tall or short? Mother or father? Single or married or divorced? Homeless or home dweller? Renter or mortgage holder? Book worm or film fan, jogger or rambler, spiritual or non-spiritual? As the list goes on (and it will), you will begin to build a more individual picture of yourself, and hopefully as you do this more fully you will have begun to recognise who you are.

Still the picture is not complete. It lacks depth. Surely we can be many of these things and they can overlap. Our identity (like our mind) is a whole, not a list of its many parts, and anyway none of these absolute categories is entirely satisfactory. Categorical ways of looking at things are too static, while we human beings are dynamic. 'We are what we do repeatedly,' according to Aristotle, so these labels allow us no room for the roll and wave of life. That is why we need other, more nuanced, more progressive ways to address the question of who we are.

One way is to include some narrative answers to the questions of our identity. By asking ourselves about our relationships and our capacities, our concerns and our limitations, we find the things that help to define us. This also helps us to look for ourselves beyond the limited categories of married/single, employed/unemployed, working age/retired and so on, to form a topographical map of ourselves, one that is more than a completed census form.

Sometimes I encourage people to use the headings of CHIME to explore and identify their unique characteristics. So, ask yourself these questions: How am I connected? Where do I source my hopes? What meaning do I have in my life and from where does my empowerment come? Answering these questions helps to build the portrait of your identity beyond a set of categories or the projections of a career path to form a rounder, more three-dimensional shape akin to a whole person.

Remember, there is no identity that is preferable. The

aim in Step Six is an authentic recognition, and it harks back to Step Three – living a more mindful life. The way of health is to foster a kinder, more compassionate you, and this is only possible by knowing who you are.

By answering these questions, a more authentic three-dimensional understanding of your identity will grow. This insight will help you to make your whole new plan for living more relevant and more sustainable by placing your identity within the story of your life. This identification could become a source of greater understanding, giving you greater compassion for what you have become and greater hope for what you can be.

So, now you have begun to answer the question 'Who am I?' You may notice that as you take this step, your description becomes something else. It becomes your history. It includes a personal recognition of many objective and subjective realities over time. It includes many other experiences, some benign, some more traumatic. In this way your recognition is becoming truly apparent to you, as a whole being living in 360 degrees.

To explain the value of this three-dimensional identification in time and space, I usually guide my patients to an image illustrating the work of psychologist Erik Erikson.[xxxix] This image shows the journey through successive stages of psychological development throughout life. At each stage of this journey, as development becomes more challenged,

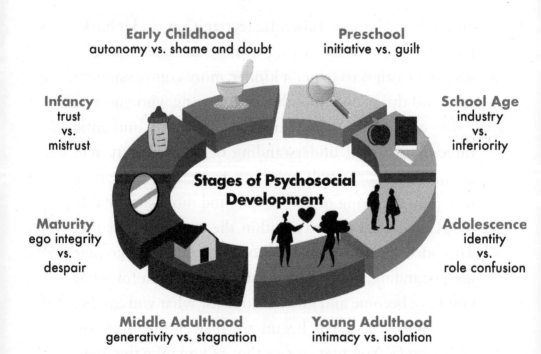

Early Childhood
autonomy vs. shame and doubt

Preschool
initiative vs. guilt

Infancy
trust
vs.
mistrust

School Age
industry
vs.
inferiority

Stages of Psychosocial Development

Maturity
ego integrity
vs.
despair

Adolescence
identity
vs.
role confusion

Middle Adulthood
generativity vs. stagnation

Young Adulthood
intimacy vs. isolation

identity becomes less about labels or categories and more about the way we negotiate life. The difficulties of the young person around autonomy and initiative are contrasted with issues of doubt, mistrust and confusion. Similarly, adulthood is characterised by challenges around intimacy, generativity and integrity, and these are underpinned by fears of isolation, stagnation and despair. Identifying these universal challenges at our particular stage of life offers us another way of considering the question of who we are. Looking at our identity in this way, we begin to see ourselves in the context of our development.

We can see that our psychological development

moves with each stage and each role in life. We need this recognition to be reflected in our unique whole new plan for living. Our unique identity is formed by a human life lived on an increasingly complex stairway. At each step of life, we are challenged by the need to reconcile ourselves to life's demands and its limits. This task of reconciliation is formative and is part of the balancing act that is so central to all our health.

Perhaps the best way I can illustrate the value of this self-identification is with a clinical example. Colin is a patient of mine. He is paraplegic, but one day he taught me that he was also many other things.

It was a difficult day for me and I was running late. I was surprised to find Colin waiting outside my room in the hospital. I had forgotten about him. He had an appointment with me, but he had been waiting for over an hour. Now he was very angry. I began our consultation by apologising to him for delaying him, but nothing I said would appease him.

'You can say what you want, but it's not about the delay,' he said. 'It's about respect for me.'

'I said I am sorry,' I replied, 'and I am.'

'That's just the point,' he said. 'As far as you're concerned, the matter is over, isn't it?'

'Yes,' I said. 'At least I hope so.'

'Well, it isn't. It would be if it wasn't so obvious to me that you don't see me for who I am.'

'I don't understand,' I said.

'I know you don't, but this delay has given me my opportunity to ask you some questions.'

'OK,' I replied.

'How do you see me? Am I Colin, that paraplegic or Colin, a man with paraplegia? To you am I just that guy in a wheelchair? Do you see me as a diagnosis or a human being? Am I a diabetic? Or am I a man with diabetes? Am I a depressive or a man who experiences depression from time to time? My question is: Who do you think I am, Dr Lucey?'

'Colin,' I said, 'please forgive and just tell me who you really are.'

'I am a human being, with a story and a life and a past and hopefully a future. You forgot that today but the truth is, so did I. Way back when I became depressed, I became invisible. Others may look at me and just see my wheelchair, but now I see myself, and I see all of me.'

'And what do you see?' I asked.

'I see a kind person, a person with rights and hopes, and even though I have my fears, I am reaching out for help and I am showing up!'

'And on time as well,' I added.

'Exactly,' he said, 'and unlike you, I have been here all the time.'

So, what more can I say? In Step Six I am asking you to move from the basic categorical descriptions of who you think you are and fill your blank page with who you know and feel that you are. Consider your dilemmas and try to identify your stage in life. Think of all of this and then ask yourself, 'Where do I want to go from here?' Seen in this way, Step Six is more than a static attempt to identify yourself. Self-identification is a means to an end, not an end in itself. It helps to describe your route to a more authentic relationship with yourself. Now it's time to accept yourself by first understanding who you really are. Before any of us can live well, we must discover the ability to love ourselves. Only then is Step Six complete – by learning to love yourself and love others just as much.

A fuller description of who and what we are helps us to ask ourselves these questions about our plan for life: questions like, 'Where do I want to be?' and 'What do I want to do?' In Step Six our answers will be very personal and also very practical.

At this point it's necessary to digress a little – to stop for a while and give ourselves some time to ponder these things. As we do this, we should find some time to consider more universal factors and learn some things about the health challenges any of us might experience. This could be a good time to go back and reconsider the best ways to live (such as those described in the five ways to wellness).

It might also be useful at this point to emphasise something else about making our new plans for living.

Plans are made but events can always get in the way: none of us knows what the future will bring. Whatever happens, this step of recognising your identity will have been helpful. Difficulties may arise, but recognising our identity will help us to build an authentic way forward. It can also help us to discover our fellowship with others by first acknowledging who we are. The next step (Step Seven) is to increase our understanding of issues that may be experienced by all human beings, whatever our identity.

Step Seven

Recognising the Social Determinants of Health

Understanding the origins of our stress and distress is the next step (Step Seven) of our whole new plan for living. With this understanding, we will augment our plan and place its emphasis where it needs to be: on the environmental factors that we can change, and the behavioural issues that we must address.

It comes as a surprise to many people that environmental and social factors play such a large role in determining our experience of stress, distress and illness. In making our whole new plan for living it's essential to understand that so much of illness is socially determined – much of our distress is the result of factors in our society, many of which seem outside our control. Gender, social class and income all play major roles. The differences between the sexes and the emergence of mental ill health in men and women illustrates this very powerfully, showing the way social and economic circumstances influence all our wellbeing. So, let's look at sex and mental health in a deeper way.

Gender and mental health

The need for a less rigid notion of gender has been highlighted by the LGBTQ community. This more diverse understanding is influenced by the recognition of more nuanced ways of self-identification through gender, race and social affiliation. Within this diversity women and men have very different experiences of mental health and wellbeing,[xl] and most of these differences are not because of their biology. They are socially determined. To fully understand this, it is necessary to acknowledge the biological differences that do exist, if only to rule them out of the discussion. So, let's consider how women and men compare in biological terms.

The major mental health difficulties, such as schizophrenia, bipolar mood disorders and obsessive-compulsive disorders (OCD), are not subject to gender bias. They occur with equal frequency in the male and the female of our species. But men are more likely than women to be diagnosed with a variety of other mental health problems and difficulties, such as antisocial personality disorder, substance misuse disorders, alcohol dependency and other addictions. Men have increased rates of autism and of attention deficit hyperactivity disorder (ADHD). They are more likely to have difficulties with stuttering, and speech and language development. They tend to have more learning disabilities and more conduct disorders. Men are more likely to complete suicide, and this is mainly because they use more violent means. To sum up, of the three biggest mental health problems in our community – depression, alcohol misuse and suicide – men are overrepresented in the latter two.

The experiences of women and men are not the same. For example, menstruation, childbirth and the menopause, and their associated mental health difficulties such as premenstrual tension and post-partum psychosis, cannot be experienced by men. Women also live longer than men and, if only for that reason, they have a higher incidence of dementia than their male counterparts.

The biological differences between women and men arise mostly from the different levels of the female hormone oestrogen; this may explain why women experience psychosis on average five years later than men. Higher levels of oestrogen appear to protect the developing brain. The female brain is also structurally different in subtle ways. These differences are most apparent in the limbic system – the cortical brain network that facilitates some of our most important cognitive and emotional functions. Within the limbic system the ratio of grey matter to white matter, the balance between thinking tissue and structural tissue, is greater in women than men. Still, these structural and biological differences in the brains of women and men are nothing when compared to their different social experiences. The major differences between women and men in terms of mental health are not biological – they are socially determined.

Women experience stress-related mental health difficulties four times more frequently than men.[xli] Depression, anxiety disorders and eating disorders are all more common among women. Women are more likely to be carers. At peak risk times for mental difficulty, women are more likely to be the sole carers of the generations who come after them as well as those who came before them. Sandwiched between these caring demands, it is women who take most responsibility in the home. All the while, women are ten times more likely to be the victim of domestic abuse or intimate partner attack. Women are still paid less than men and they are at greater risk of discrimination if they have a mental health difficulty.

These cultural and gender differences may be shifting, and there are those who fear these changes.

Some even see traditional masculinity as being in crisis, but most agree that men need to address their more destructive impulses and learn to increase their capacity for compassion, optimism and resilience. These capacities are the intimate skills that shape our ability to live well, whatever our gender.

All of this harks back to Step Six of our plan. Whatever our self-identification, however we see ourselves, we need to learn newer and better ways of living well with each other, in more loving and accepting ways. Greater tolerance of ourselves and each other is an important part of our journey to better health. It is key to Step Seven of our whole new plan for living.

Institutional abuse and our whole new plan for living

Today's conversation about health and wellness occurs in a very different context to the past. Our health challenges are timeless, but today's demand for wellbeing arises in a twenty-first-century context with a new and vivid awareness of institutional abuse.

Over the thirty years I have been working in mental healthcare, I have seen nearly every institutional authority discredited to some extent. In Ireland and across the world, the banks, churches, governments and health services have been exposed for their failures. The effects of their abuses have been palpable, painful, individual and collective.

The initial response from those in power or authority is always denial. We have all been witnesses to this. These denials inevitably lead to further delays and these add further layers to the pain of those with an experience of abuse, neglect or assault – most frequently women and children. The result is cynicism. Now it seems naive to put our trust in institutions: our collective capacity for trust has been lost. The denial of institutional abuse was predictable, even understandable. It's defensive – we all recoil from distressing revelations. Institutions are human organisations, so their reactions are similarly reflexive, like pulling a hand from a hot stove. Still, collective denial is another reason for our individual frustration and anxiety. While scapegoating of individuals is not helpful, real responsibility needs to be acknowledged before we can heal.

The experiences of institutional failure continue to contribute to our collective unease. The truth may one day set us free, but not quickly. The awareness of our vulnerability may even paralyse us for a time. Hearing the truth is painful, but it is essential. It's the beginning of our recovery. We will need to hear much more of it before we can fully reconcile ourselves to our collective past and to our present and to each other.

Step Seven of our whole new plan for living includes this exercise of reconciliation. The restoration of our health and wellness must be our priority. Surely a genuine commitment to human rights, to justice and to peace is not too much to ask from those in power or authority? This healing process can only really begin when we make these commitments to each other. This will require the fullest telling of it all so that we can begin to understand the denial of it all. Our investment in redress has been too narrow. For the abusers and the abused, justice and recovery should be the goals. This will require more than a prison sentence, or financial compensation or dispatch to a therapist. My view is that a cultural re-evaluation is necessary. Perhaps we need a 'truth and reconciliation commission' as took place in South Africa after the end of the apartheid system, or, even better, something akin to the German cultural exploration which followed the revelation of the atrocities of the Holocaust. The Germans made a special word for this process of reconciliation. They called it *Vergangenheitsbewältigung* – acknowledging the past in order to come to terms with it in the present. For many people, this healing cannot come soon enough.

Stigma and our whole new plan for living

Stigma refers to the negative way those with mental health disorders are treated by society. Stigma is always a negative experience and its malign influence is evident in education and employment. Whether or not to disclose a mental health problem is one of the most challenging questions for recovery. It comes up day after day. We discussed this in Step Four – managing our health in difficult situations (see page 93).

People like to believe that the influence of stigma is diminishing. There are more people talking about mental health in the media and in political spheres; plenty of high-profile figures are 'coming out' with interviews and books about their mental health challenges. But the reality is somewhat different if you happen to be the person with the mental health problem.

Stigma goes deeper than we realise. Our awareness may be growing, but the time has come to move that awareness into action about our mental health, and our whole new plan for living would be a better place to start. Stigma is a barrier to recovery. The reactions of our family, friends and neighbours are good illustrations of the way stigma works. How many of us would honestly want to rely on someone after learning that they'd had a mental health episode? Would we behave the same way even if we knew that someone had recovered from a breakdown? Would you go out on a date with a person who once had a mental health difficulty? Would you hire someone with a history of mental health difficulties? Would you let someone with a past mental health problem babysit your children? We already know the answer to these questions. Research[xlii] tells us that, for most people, the answer would be 'no'.

Maybe it's time to call on people to live in a more enlightened way, by highlighting the scale of the losses to our society caused by the stigma around mental health. The economic losses come from absenteeism and presenteeism (being at work when unwell because it's not possible to disclose) and through a sheer waste of human resources. A recent OECD report[xliii] found that the loss to a society of untreated mental health difficulties equates to around 4 per cent of gross domestic product (GDP). In Ireland, that amounts to more than €8 billion every year. For an anti-stigma appeal to succeed, we must make it clear that mental healthcare could be effective, but in my experience practically no one believes this to be the case. Although modern therapy interventions for people in mental health need are very effective, many people just don't believe that recovery is possible. The failure to make greater investment in health services is hardly surprising. We are left in 'catch-22' territory – as services haven't been commissioned and sufficiently resourced, people don't have timely access to high-quality mental health services and therefore to the possibility of recovery. Consequently, people can't believe in the value of services that in many cases don't exist and in others cannot be accessed.

Many people fear the prospect of revealing their mental health difficulties to others, believing this revelation will damage them. For many years, I have gone around the country, to schools and colleges, offices and factories – anywhere that will have me – to promote mental health awareness. Many people do this kind of health awareness promotion, including other service providers and service users. In my talks I used to tackle stigma head-on by asking the audience to put their hands up if they, like me, had at least one family member going through mental health difficulty. I believed this appeal was a reasonable one, since the data tells us that every family has at least one person in mental distress at any given time.[xliv] Nevertheless, invariably, when I would ask for this show of solidarity, no hands would go up. No one would acknowledge their family mental health history in public. Sometimes, people would come up to me after my presentation to apologise and quietly reveal their story. 'I couldn't say it out there,' they would say, 'you can understand.'

Recently, I told this story to the broadcaster Abie Philbin Bowman. He was contributing to our mental health initiative on the St Patrick's Hospital pop-up radio station as part of the anti-stigma campaign known as 'Walk in My Shoes Radio'.

'Ah, I get it,' said Abie. 'Why don't you reverse the question? Ask them to put their hands up if they don't have a family member in mental distress. See what happens then.'

I have used Abie Bowman's strategy ever since and

it has worked. Now, when I put the question to the audience no hands go up, and everyone looks around. They realise what has happened: that when it comes to mental health, all our families are in this together. Some have greater needs than others, but no family is entirely spared, at least not for long.

So, how can we tackle the problem of stigma?

The answer is not simple. We still have a long way to go before we are truly free of this deeply damaging phenomenon, but there are some hopeful international examples of triumph over stigma, which should encourage us. A favourite of mine is the story of the Norwegian prime minister,[xlv] who resigned from his post following calls from the opposition to step down after he disclosed that he was in treatment for depression. A general election ensued, but the Norwegian people returned the prime minister with an even bigger majority and their economy grew over the following years because of his prudent management. Norway avoided the dreaded cycle of boom and bust that befell the rest of Europe. The people trusted him, and this trust was not diminished by his disclosure of mental illness. The Norwegian people were not stigmatic and actually trusted him more as a result of his honesty.

It's a story of hope. These things can improve, but overcoming this battle is still the biggest societal hurdle we have in the fight for better mental health.

The environment and our whole new plan

There are many forms of pollution in our world; the most enduring forms are the ones we barely even notice. Take for example the issue of light pollution. Our world has become wide-eyed, vigilant and constantly on alert. One consequence is that our sleep has deteriorated. Another is that we have lost our appreciation of the darkness.

Our urban environment is awake twenty-four hours a day. As a result, the quality of our sleep is suffering, making us more irritable, less effective, less contented and less healthy than we would otherwise be. Increasing our awareness of the importance of sleep was part of Step Two of our whole new plan for living (see page 50). And there are many other reasons for our loss of sleep, now we have smartphones, computers, and twenty-four-hour TV. The world doesn't stop for bedtime anymore. Our towns and cities, our homes and our workplaces are permanently illuminated, and we live in a world saturated with artificial light. The 'starry sky at night' is no longer visible in many of our cities. Light pollution is a reality. Darkness is seen as something abhorrent, except, perhaps, in the wilderness. Despite all this illumination though, we are in the dark and more afraid.

We need to re-evaluate our dark environment. To restore our sleep, we could start by reconsidering our domestic attitude to darkness. Let's ask ourselves some 'illuminating' questions. Do our homes need to be lit up permanently like Christmas trees? Would our evenings become more peaceful if we chose to adopt a more restful style of lighting in the spaces we share? This brightness is confusing our brains. We have already agreed in Step Two that we need to prioritise our sleep, so let's restore our night-time. Let's turn down the lights.

There are many reasons to be concerned for our environment (and light pollution is only one of them). Rising temperatures, rising tides and melting glaciers are real jeopardies for us, and the reason I pick out this example of pollution is because it is indicative. This is an example of an environmental pollution with potential mental health consequences. The environment is still an abstract concern for many people. Damage to our habitat is harming us in ways we don't sufficiently appreciate. This harm is both physical and mental. We need to examine our environmental issues in a new health-centred way. It's not just a question of turning down the lights. It's about learning to CHIME with the connectedness

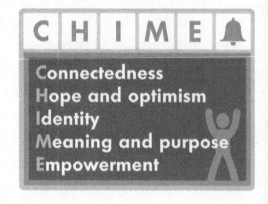

C H I M E

Connectedness
Hope and optimism
Identity
Meaning and purpose
Empowerment

of things (see page 216 for more on this acronym for things that define our success).

No constructive enterprise, however profitable in the short term, can be good for our society if it's harmful to our environment, to us and to our health. Whenever we look at our initiatives in economics or politics, industry or agriculture, Step Seven of our whole new plan for living means we will choose to prioritise a 'whole of health' perspective and make our initiatives CHIME. A genuine 'whole of health' analysis could be transformative. A sustainable enterprise is one that is good for the 'whole of health'. This understanding of the priority of the whole of health underpins our whole new plan for living.

Public health investment and our whole new plan for living

Most illness arises in the context of external stress, brought about by forces in our society or in the environment that have the potential to destabilise us. COVID-19 is the most pressing example but it is not the first. Infectious diseases such as diphtheria, measles, tuberculosis and polio were all commonplace and, in many countries, still are. The lesson learned from them is that our health status and our wellness is societal and environmental. This truth is not just about infections. More illness is caused by homelessness, bad housing, illiteracy and poverty than we are prepared to acknowledge. In Step One of our whole new plan we recognised this. This is why our new plans for living are shared concerns. The stresses that have the greatest impact upon our health are most commonly collective. To make a success of our whole new plan for living, we need to consider the environment in which we live and the quality of the lives we share.

Improving the health of society could be a national goal. Building a healthier population could be our greatest achievement. For too long, our economic ambitions have been focused exclusively on our 'growth', without a real idea of our 'wealth'. But real wealth is health. Nations need growth, but growth is only sustainable in a healthy context.

We are human, so we are social. Our individual health is enabled by our shared wellbeing. It will be impossible to ensure our individual health if we disregard the health of those around us. The dividends arising from a healthier society will be for everyone.

This is why population-health investments are the foundations of all good healthcare systems. Societies that ensure the availability of these basics of public health are more likely to be good places to live, to work and to love. These health investments can make healthy living and economic growth possible for more and more people, and that's good for everyone.

Improved public health begins long before a person is seen in a hospital or a clinic. Investments in public health extend across neighbourhoods and communities and throughout the environment. These shared investments in health include cleaner air and water, proper sanitation, equitable systems of justice, better access to childcare, education and housing, universal immunisation and community safety. These investments in a healthier society yield far more per head than any other capital investment in medicine or surgery. That's good for people and it's good for the economy. It's a mistake to divide the two. Economic growth and personal wellbeing will be sustained by this 'whole of health' analysis. This leads us on to another truth: there is no sustainable economy without a health economy.

The benefits of almost any medical treatment are negligible when compared to the gains achieved through these population-health measures. Throughout history, on every continent, in men and in women, the biggest gains in health and wellness have arisen from investments in peace, justice, equality and shared prosperity. By contrast to these, poverty and war have been the biggest sources of illness and disease since the beginning of recorded time. A healthy, thriving modern society is not just about the economy; it is about a healthy economy. For many years health spending has been regarded as a drain on the economy. But in Step Seven of our whole new plan for living, we will begin to see that health investment is a driver of personal and economic growth, not a drain on it.

This investment needs to be strategically planned and focused on population health.

Very few illnesses arise from issues completely beyond our knowledge. Medical science has become extraordinarily effective and informative about the best ways to restore our health and to maintain our wellbeing. So, why do we ignore these data when it comes to our health investment? Perhaps because we misunderstand population health and our wellness.

In the richest countries in the world, health spending has become unbalanced. It is not determined by public health science. In 2019 my country, Ireland, spent more than €17 billion on healthcare (out of the government's total revenue of just over €50 billion). Only a small share of this was spent on public health and mental health, and yet these areas are the most likely to yield general health benefits. Preventative healthcare investment amounted to less than €0.6 billion. Instead, interventions likely to deliver the lowest societal health yield (like hospital building and individual treatments) got the lion's share of Ireland's healthcare investment.

The failure to invest in public health can become a personal matter very quickly. Public health is a very abstract concept until an illness like COVID-19 hits your own door and we find access to intensive care is more difficult than we imagined. We may always have known where our local clinic was, at least vaguely. We may have been happy to talk to a GP or a nurse, but who would have thought that one day we might have difficulty accessing intensive care?

The same is true for most people accessing mental healthcare. In this arena, most of us are in the dark: this is true even in the wealthiest of nations. In the USA, 60 per cent of youth with major depression did not receive any mental health treatment in 2017–2018.[xlvi] So, in the richest country the world has ever known, the most common response to mental health problems is no treatment at all.

A consensus on healthcare investment in our modern world is hard to achieve. Many other factors outside the scientific data influence our decision-making processes. Fear and stigma are influential, pessimism and poverty are there too, but politics and power are also huge sources of distortion when it comes to rational investment in healthcare.

A good example comes from a current controversy in Ireland regarding the building of a National Children's Hospital. This much-needed facility has been on the government's agenda for many years. Now, the final cost of this hospital will be far in excess of the original €0.5 billion estimate – the current estimate is closer to €2 billion. This makes the National Children's Hospital of Ireland one of the most expensive hospital developments in world history. There seems no limit to the amounts of money we are prepared to spend on some hospital healthcare projects and this is at the cost of more valuable population health.

Even when the children's hospital is up and running, not one extra child will be cared for. In terms of bang for our buck, this health spending is just not rational. We forget that hospitals have little influence on our general health and wellbeing – as the cost of the hospital capital rises, there is less to spend on health prevention in the community. As far as numbers of children are concerned, the National Children's Hospital is already a self-defeating exercise.

Obviously, governments have to make difficult decisions and must take many factors into account. Theirs is a heavy burden of responsibility, but if public health spending was more rational, and more influenced by the scientific data, we might spend our money differently. The voting public would need to be on board.

Perhaps it's time for a new consensus about our healthcare investment. Where should governments spend our money on healthcare? Should it be spent on better public health, primary care and mental health? Health spending by governments is often represented as a percentage of GDP[xlvii] but this measure (although rising) means very little to most people and it tells us very little about the costs of healthcare as a share of our total revenue. If we represented our healthcare spending as a proportion of our income, a clearer picture would emerge. Expenditure on healthcare in Ireland (total includes state and private spend) was €22.5 billion in 2018. The direct cost to the public purse that year was €17 billion out of a total revenue of roughly €50 billion and total income tax returns of around €21 billion.[xlviii] This analysis reveals that our healthcare system is costing almost every cent we earn in income tax. Assuming there is no more growth in revenue, something will have to be done – but what? Step Seven of our whole new plan has the answer: what is needed now is a redirection of our health spending towards population health and mental health.

The post-war consensus around a universal health franchise is not likely to return. The rise of populism in many of the richest countries, for example the UK and the USA, makes opposition to central management of healthcare more likely – not less. The experience of the Affordable Care Act (Obamacare) is one example, even though the arguments against public health investment have already been challenged and in many ways overturned by the COVID-19 pandemic. The pandemic has driven even some right-wing governments to spend more money, illustrating the fact that dismissive references to the role of the 'nanny state' were never driven by health data or public health reality.

In our new plan for living our health is not entirely in our hands. What we need in Step Seven is recognition of this fact. Healthcare spending needs a 'whole of health' analysis and it needs leadership guided by scientific data. This science will help us to grow collectively stronger and more resilient. In Step Seven we will look for better leadership to promote better access to childcare, education, housing and social competency, and to build societal recovery through promotion of human rights and positive values. In this whole new plan for living, the five ways to wellness (see page 9) would be paramount, and so our collective talents and interests, our friendships and neighbourhoods would be seen as just as important as our taxes and our industry. The positive indicators of our health would be as important as the strength of our market sentiment. This may not be your plan, at least not yet, but let's agree on some things. Market growth is built on sentiment, and sentiment is an illusion. The potential for social wellbeing is not an illusion. Recovery does not have to be a fairytale. We could make economic health a reality if we invested more in public health.

If as a society we fail to invest in the collective sources of good health, we are in for a collective nightmare. Investment in these shared domains of resilience is required to enable us to live longer, healthier and more productive lives. A culture of health could make us stronger, more resilient and more economically successful. Leadership dedicated to this vision could achieve a great new deal. Hopefully in these times of difficulty, our leadership will see that the right thing to do for our economy is the healthy thing.

Put simply, our health spending is out of control. It is not only our inability to control its costs that causes the imbalance. We lack the rational ability to consider the value of our health spending. This point has been made elegantly by Harvard professor Michael Porter with his healthcare investment equation.

Porter's Value Equation[xlix] considers the relationships between three elements of healthcare experience: the quality of the service (Q), the volume of service (V) and the costs (C). Porter proposes that value in healthcare is a quantifiable parameter, and since it is a measurable, defined one, it should be possible to manage it. For Porter, healthcare value is equal to Q multiplied by S and divided by C.

Value in Healthcare $= (Q \times S)/C$

This is a mathematical expression of a utilitarian principle. In other words, Porter is suggesting that our healthcare spend should be about doing the most good for the most people. If our healthcare decisions were based on this measurable parameter, a more rational and transparent health service might emerge. Certainly, our spending would look very different. One way to manage our investments would be to apply this utilitarian parameter proposed by Porter. Perhaps, that way, the reluctance of the few to pay for the welfare of many might be mitigated.

So in Step Seven of our whole new plan for living we need to ask ourselves some questions about our health spending. In our whole new plan, who takes responsibility for our health? When I ask myself this question I keep coming back to the same answer. Responsibility for healthcare must be balanced. It must be shared and the answer must include greater collaboration. To me this makes undeniable public health sense. It also makes economic sense.

Individuals cannot simply choose to be well. We must support each other to live well. Since we all live together, our collective health matters to all of us. Surely COVID-19 has taught us this. In our new plan for living, we need to modify our sense of independence and recognise our inter-dependence. Life is stressful for everyone, but life is also unequal and unfair. In our whole new plan, we will rediscover the value of our collective health, and work towards the rebalancing of health for each other. We need to learn to make better collective choices, if only for our self-interest. There is an old African saying often quoted by the Jesuit priest Fr Peter McVerry:[1] 'If my neighbour is hungry, then my chickens are not safe.' If it were only for our own good, we need to recognise the needs of our fellow human beings.

The same is true of our mental health. People with the most severe mental health difficulties are dying on average twenty years earlier than their peers.

They are the most neglected part of our society. The consequences of this inequality are greater loss to our economy, more illness and earlier death.

In Step Seven of our whole new plan we need to ensure that more people will have the opportunity to live a mentally healthy life. This will require more buy-in from each one of us. Healthy initiatives are not pie in the sky: they require greater access to safe food and housing, universal immunisation and proper sanitation, clean water and environmental security, freedom from injustice, and better opportunities for employment. In the twenty-first century are these too much to ask? These basics are the real fundamentals of health that enable our healthy lives. If implemented, they would result in a healthier, fitter, better-off society.

Caring for yourself when caring for someone else

Every family in the land has at least one thing in common. Whether we know it or not, at least one member of our family will have a mental health difficulty in our lifetime (see Step Five). This universal truth is deeply shocking to many people. It's another stigma thing. It comes up daily in the clinic, especially when I ask a person in distress whether there is any history of mental health difficulty in their family. The most common response is flat denial.

Since every family in the land has someone with a mental health difficulty, there is no use in dismissing this response. Instead, I try to use the problem to learn a little more.

'So, do you talk about these things in your family?' I ask.

'No, never, why would we? I mean ... it never comes up.'

Denial is not a conscious response. It's not the same as a lie. It may be that someone has no knowledge of their family history, but this is a far cry from healthy insight. For example, a more accurate answer to the question of family history might be:

'No, there is no family history of mental health difficulty. At least none that I am aware of.'

Awareness at the time of any mental health challenge is important. This is demonstrated every day by families caring for someone with an enduring difficulty. Many of these carers know that recovery grows through greater collaboration and more fellowship, but this needs greater openness. We can have no shame about our mental health or about our need for caring.

We need to prepare, and to understand the challenges faced by carers. Health is a societal concern. We depend on our carers. We need to sustain our carers as well as those they care for. It is often difficult for family members to articulate their own needs, but most caring is done within families and it can be demanding work.

In Step Seven this is not going to be easy, but making our whole new plan for living will mean learning new caring skills. For families in acute need, this could mean learning the ability to listen and to go on listening.

So, is it possible to make a whole new plan for yourself when you're caring for someone else? My answer is a definite 'yes'. Self-care is an essential basis for our whole new plan, especially if you are already caring for someone else. Now is the time to start, by taking better care of ourselves. If you are a carer, it's worth taking this initiative to mind yourself.

Here is a list of some suggestions I regularly make to my patients, and most especially to their carers. These are some of the most practical things you can do, and they could become part of your whole new plan for living. They arise from the five ways to wellness and the eight dimensions of health. You will see that all successful health initiatives CHIME.

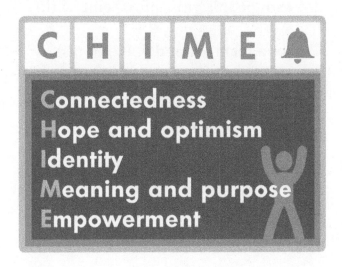

1. Remember, your health is your priority.

2. Look for support and take it.

3. Keep connected to your friends – isolation makes life more difficult.

4. Keep exercising – even five minutes more each day is worthwhile.

5. Make your sleep a priority.

6. Speak up for yourself: remember, it's OK to say that you're not OK.

7. Give yourself a break (actually, lots of breaks).

8. Make some time to do the things you like to do, with people you enjoy being with.

9. Gather a team around you. No task is sustainable on your own. Look for fellowship collaboration and support from other people in the same situation.

10. Prepare for the long term. Live in the short term.

Hope

One thing above all else is essential for this step of our new plan. It is hope. Hope is an essential feature of CHIME and so for this reason alone we need greater optimism. Nothing perpetuates suffering like pessimism. Where there is no hope, there can be no constructive plan, no therapeutic action and therefore no potential for recovery.

In my area of mental health this pessimism is deep. Unfortunately, negativity about mental healthcare goes unnoticed in our community, and mostly unchallenged by our leadership, and so negativity regarding our mental health becomes self-fulfilling. Negativity has a very damaging impact on the provision of better mental healthcare, and it works both ways. Investment in public health and in mental healthcare has been limited for a very long time. Poor investment limits the possibility for better results. Poor results limit the likelihood of greater investment. That is why public health and mental health have been the poor relations of our health services for so many years.

Hope restores us to reality. This statement is not naive or self-deceiving. Our response to the COVID-19 pandemic showed this to be true. We were right to sustain our hope. Now we have a duty to each other to ensure our hope was justified, recognising that our hopes for health and for recovery come from our shared commitment to mutual wellbeing. When we share this hope, we will sustain our health and support our collective return to health.

These are the facts. Recovery is the most frequent outcome from illness, and this is also true for those with mental health difficulties. Our belief in recovery is not a fad. It is not a flash in the pan. So our hope is a belief and it is supported by the evidence, and this hope is the basis of our whole new plan for living. Hope helps us to sustain our whole new plan for living and the long and complex journey to recovery. Hope enables us to manage more than one set of risks at one time. Hope helps us to live with better balance and to limit the risk of relapse. Hope helps us to live well.

We need this hope. The biggest health problems for human beings in the future will inevitably be those created by human beings. Take for example our growing awareness of environmental damage across our world. These hazards are increased by our behaviours, our actions that disregard our shared need for a healthy environment. We know that human illness and suffering will continue to be about two things: the damage we do to each other and the harm we are doing to our world. So hope is the only way.

It used to be said that a doctor's role was 'seldom to cure, but always to reassure'. In modern times, many of us have come to believe that giving reassurance is giving 'false hope'. We demand that our professionals are more precautionary, so they give us the grimmest forecast and nothing but the grim forecast. Unfortunately, this 'precautionary' approach has had some unforeseen problems. Our anxiety is increasing. Misuse of the precautionary approach has come to mean that hope is left out of the story, even though hope is essential for our recovery. Any treatment given in the absence of hope is bound to fail.

Obviously giving false reassurance would be an abuse, but the practice of reassurance should not be misunderstood. It is not false or abusive to be reassuring and hopeful. We become less resilient, not more so, without reassurance and hope. In our new plan, we need to support some bolder human qualities like courage, persistence and determination. The ability to give and receive reassurance is still necessary, since panic is our persistent enemy. When anxiety comes in this crescendo form, we can be overwhelmed, becoming more risk-averse and less engaged in our life and our recovery.

That is why in our whole new plan for living we will never deny these hopeful truths: all things pass, and only love endures. We cannot sacrifice hope on the altar of total disclosure. Genuine reassurance is as truthful as it is essential for life. Genuine disclosure must include access to better information about the challenges to our health. We need better ways to share the data about our opportunities for recovery and for a longer and more fulfilling life. Better information will help us to strike a balance between healthy and unhealthy patterns of living. The evidence is that with better data, we make better choices. The way to overcome our fear is to overcome our ignorance about our health and our life. The truth will make us well, especially when it is shared with hope.

The hope for health and wellness is that we will become better informed and better equipped. We will CHIME. As we come to know the data, we will choose to live accordingly. The next generation will be better informed. They will choose better ways to live. There is hope in this. With this hope we will be able to take the next step – Step Eight – moving from stress and distress to recovery and a better life.

Moving from Stress and Distress to Recovery

Stress is an inevitable part of life. We will all experience difficulties and hopefully we will cope with most of them. This stress in our lives, in our families and our friends is not evenly distributed, but there is a very clear relationship between stress and poor health. As we have seen in the steps so far, difficulties at home and at work – with various losses in our lives and in our relationships – are universal, but they are not evenly spread. The evidence is that more stressful lives tend to be more distressed. These associations are complex and still poorly understood, but stress is a major contributor to the most common human diseases, including depression, cardiovascular disease,[li] cancer and even infectious diseases like COVID-19. Obviously infectious diseases are caused by pathogens such as bacteria, fungi and viruses, and so they are not simply caused by stress, but stress exacerbates the course and morbidity of every disease. In our whole new plan for living we aim to rebalance our stress with fresh strategies for living and greater awareness of the need for action. Step Eight of our plan is about practical ways of moving from stress and distress to recovery and a better life.

The damaging effects of stress are psychological, biological and social. Stress affects our hormonal systems, especially by involving the panic hormone adrenalin and the stress hormone cortisol. The toxic consequences of excessive stresses are manifest throughout the body and the brain, making many illnesses worse.[lii] Psychological effects of stress impact our cognitive responses, and the social effects of stress lead to a deterioration in our lifestyle, with poor self-care and increased risk-taking behaviours. It's beyond doubt that too much stress is bad for us.

And yet not all stress is associated with poor health. Most people survive under stress and they remain well. They cope, they adapt, and they carry on. Just as stress is unevenly distributed, so the ability to cope with stress is not evenly present in our community. The facts of health and wellness apply here too: economic status, lifestyle and genetic background all have a bearing on our ability to adapt to stress.

Coping with stress requires a whole-body and whole-brain response. In Step Eight of our whole new plan for living we will look at stress from biological, social and psychological points of view. We will acknowledge the inevitability of stress, but our plan will help us to overcome it. Our strategy is to harness our healthy skills for living and to learn how to survive and to live well. This step will require a more personal inventory of our stresses to make changes that will help us to recover, and learn from others' experience. We can discover new ways to thrive.

Exceptionally stressful experiences are sometimes referred to as major life events.

The five most stressful major life events are:

1. Death of a loved one

2. Divorce, or relationship breakdown

3. Moving to a new house

4. Major illness or injury

5. Job loss

It's important to understand the meaning and significance of each type of stress for us. For example, stress can threaten us at deep levels by jeopardising our continuity, our connectivity and our integrity. Some stresses are threats to our continuity (like major illness), and some are losses to our connectivity (like a job loss or the death of someone close), and some are the deepest attacks on our personal integrity (like violent assault, coercive control or rape). Some stresses represent forms of personal rejection; others are associated with feelings of fear and uncertainty and ultimately loss of control. Stress can lead to the re-emergence of previous traumas and this re-experiencing increases the difficulty of current stressful life events for us.

Stress is not always episodic and there is evidence that continuing stress may be more damaging than episodic major life events. The continual stress of caring for someone with dementia is a common example. Everyday hassles (or so-called minor life events) are also frequent sources of stress. Examples include such commonplace problems as a car breaking down or increasing demands at work or minor legal difficulties. Cumulatively these minor life events may also be damaging to our health, especially when they are persistent, unresolved or unmitigated by social support.

Whether stress occurs in the context of persistent minor difficulties or occasional major life events, the hazardous result is the phenomenon we call 'distress'. This is a painful reaction to stress. It is a universal experience and it is inevitable at some stage in our lives. There is an important distinction to be made between stress and distress. While stress is potentially good for us, distress is never helpful. A problem is a distressed reaction to a stressful life event. The question we ask in Step Eight is: how do we know when our stress is turning into distress?

Increased awareness is our best tool to help us recognise when our stress is turning things upside-down. The first seven steps of our whole new plan all point to this greater self-awareness. In our whole new plan for living, we have learned to recognise when our sleep is under attack, when we have lost our appetite for life, when our patience is being used up, and when we're no longer able to laugh. In Step Eight we acknowledge that when these things are happening to us our stress has turned into our distress. With Step Eight of our whole new plan for living we take the time to act for a better life.

Some people find maintaining this self-awareness a particularly difficult challenge. Some members of Alcoholics Anonymous, for example, are reminded of their need to manage stress by referring to the acronym 'HALT'. This encourages us to recognise when we are hungry, angry, lonely or tired. In other words, it's a way of acknowledging when and why we are stressed and giving us space to do something about it. In our plan we will remember that it's OK to ask ourselves questions like 'When was I last OK?' and 'Why am I not OK now?' The answer is invariably related to the experience of stress and distress.

Step Eight of our whole new plan for living means planning to undo these painful reactions to stress and making changes to resolve our distress. Our new strategy means learning to adapt to stress and to overcome our most distressful experiences. This may not be easy. Some people find the process of adaptation to stress much more difficult than others. There is evidence that stressful life events in childhood can make adult adaptation to stress much more challenging, but the adult adaptation to stress is not necessarily determined by our childhood experience. The ability to cope with stress and to mitigate our distress varies among people and across time.

Some people struggle to move beyond their painful experience of distress and so they become incapacitated for a time. I call this extra-distressful experience a 'mental breakdown'. A 'breakdown' is a time of serious mental health difficulty. In my view, a 'breakdown' is the least stigmatic term we can use to describe this temporary but complete loss of mental health. What the term 'breakdown' lacks in specificity, it gains in simplicity and universality. It is non-judgemental. Nearly everyone knows someone who has had a mental breakdown, and these experiences rarely happen out of the blue. They occur in the context of stress and distress, and they are distressing.

Unfortunately, we still feel unable to talk about the experience of mental breakdown in an open way. This silence means we don't talk enough about the effects of stress in everyday life and its potential for impaired mental health. It also means that we don't talk about the potential for recovery. Throughout my professional life I have known many people who have recovered from a mental breakdown. Believe me. Even at these times of most serious collapse there is more hope of recovery than we acknowledge. Professional intervention will be essential at this stage. No one can 'pull themselves together' from a breakdown, but it's important to remain more hopeful and to remember that even in a 'breakdown', with the right help, a recovery is the most likely outcome.

So, stress and distress are phenomena in all our lives that occur when our lives go out of balance. They can either enable our adaptation to life or disable our function in it (and they may even lead us to a breakdown). By making Step Eight part of our whole new plan for living we will be gathering our more adaptive responses and harnessing our opportunities for wellness. These can bring life to us. In Step Eight of our whole new plan for living we will see our stress as an opportunity to improve.

Let's consider Step Eight in more detail. This is a time for you to identify your individual remedies, consciously informed by what we have learned in Steps One to Seven. Your plan will grow through a better understanding of your stress and distress, helping you to live in a healthy way and shifting your thinking away from the pressures that bear down on you. It's a good time to return to your blank page (see pages 15–17), and to identify on it your stresses and distresses. By making these stresses explicit like this, your awareness and your self-compassion will grow. This acknowledgement is part of a therapeutic process. This self-compassion is part of your listening conversation with others and especially with yourself. The result will be a greater clarity and kinder understanding of your individual challenges. From that acknowledgement will come greater understanding and more commitment to your challenge.

The insights that many people gain from this step of their plan are personal and they are valuable. The same will be true for you. To illustrate this progress, it's time to share with you some insights born out of others' therapeutic journeys, people who have already made a whole new plan for living. I have rooted each of these insights in a saying, a quote, from each patient. I call these observations 'the facts of stress and distress', although they are not 'facts' in the technical sense. They are lessons taught to me by my best teachers –

my patients. They are learned through the experience of stress and distress. The survivors of difficult experiences acquire a personal form of expertise which can be shared. It's how they carry on and, ultimately, how they recover.

Hopefully you will find these insights helpful as part of Step Eight of your process. Of course, it is not possible to generalise about our distress. The facts of your distress are yours alone and they may be known only to you, but by putting your stress and distress down on paper at this stage you are giving yourself an opportunity to reflect and to plan your own response. And by considering your stress in terms of others' experiences, you will be able to learn from others and understand how they have succeeded by making a whole new plan for living.

The facts of stress

The first fact of stress

'You can't avoid stress.'

Stress cannot be avoided. And anyway, avoidance doesn't help. Stress is not an illness; it is part of life. It must be managed, and hopefully we can learn to cope with it. We may even grow through stress and learn more. Without some stress in our lives, we will not learn.

Recognising that our stress cannot be avoided is

helpful because this brings us closer to a remedy. Our whole new plan for living is an authentic approach and it includes an understanding of when and where to get professional help. At times of great stress it's important to accept help. So take inspiration from something one of my recovered patients said to me back in Step Five: 'My breakdown has become my breakthrough.' The same thing could be true for you.

The second fact of stress

'First of all, stay calm.'

No one copes with stress while being in a panic. In our whole new plan, we will learn to stay calm.

A panic attack is a crescendo of anxiety caused by the outpouring of stress hormones in the body. This crescendo may be prompted by some known stress or even by some unconscious, hidden one. Either way, a panic attack suddenly disables our defences and makes our mind and our body incapable of responding constructively. Panic makes us freeze. With the restoration of calmness, we begin to engage more constructively. Useful things just don't get done when we are in a panic; we move too quickly from 'fright' to 'fight' and ultimately, we take 'flight'. There is nothing constructive about panic.

A calm response is hard when your adrenalin is pumping, your heart is pounding, you feel like you are about to collapse. It may seem impossible when you are confronted with this seemingly catastrophic reality, but awareness through 'full catastrophic living'[liii] is recommended by mindfulness experts. This makes sense. We need to understand that a more mindful response is not a denial of what is happening. It's not a panic. It consists of a calmer engagement with stress and distress.

The third fact of stress

'All stress is personal.'

Stress is subjective. This fact is a difficult one to accept. It's hardcore stress and distress management. At this stage in our whole new plan we must go there. I don't usually talk about this third fact at the start of a therapeutic conversation. Trust is needed before we understand the personal, but as healing comes to each person, this discovery is inevitably made.

I am not recommending that you dismiss subjective experience as part of your whole new plan for living. We feel distress within ourselves because that is where the meaning of it is. In Austrian neurologist Viktor Frankl's great work *Man's Search for Meaning*,[liv] he described the value of understanding this personal meaning. Knowing your meaning, understanding the personal significance of things, can be the difference between survival and death, between coping and not coping. In Frankl's view, no one can take away the power that comes from your meaning.

The recovered become well because they discover what is meaningful to them. This is the hardest part – it is the compassionate acceptance of subjective reality, finding and loving the meaningful reality of your life. This meaning gives us the licence to be well.

The fourth fact of stress

'No one wants pity.'

Stress calls for empathy, not just sympathy, or pity. Empathy is the ability to put yourself in someone else's shoes, to try to feel someone else's pain. And empathy is challenging stuff. This is not just a matter of saying, 'Oh yes, I remember when I was going through that same experience you are having.' Sympathy such as this may be well intentioned but it's not the same as empathy.

Real empathy means trying to feel something with someone else, while knowing that someone else's feelings are subjective and unique. It is about putting yourself at the service of someone else's experience in a completely humane, egalitarian and compassionate way.

In the 1950s, American psychologist Carl Rogers identified this gift of empathy as an essential part of the therapeutic relationship.[lv] He called this 'unconditional positive regard', and he advocated what he called 'active listening' by responding in a truly compassionate way. According to Rogers, this 'regard' is more powerful than advice, because it's about experiencing a compassionate relationship. One can be empathic, and one can experience empathy. The beneficial effect is the restoration of a loving relationship with one's self through the unconditional positive regard of others. No one can be 'debated' into a more positive attitude to their stress. In my experience, when the distressed recover their health, it is not because they have found a new external reality; it's because they have found a new regard for themselves. And this only comes from empathy.

This new regard may be so completely unfamiliar that it comes as a source of surprise. The older, darker views begin to seem less negative. A life that was once isolated and burdened by guilt or shame can become reconnected and free.

To witness this recovery is to rejoice with someone else. The achievement of such a recovery is a triumph that belongs to the person who has recovered, and when someone becomes well, it is completely to their credit. The joy of being well transforms subjective experience in whole new, unforeseen ways.

The fifth fact of stress

'Stress is a whole experience involving the mind and body.'

We learned this in Step Two and Step Three. We need to look after the whole of ourselves especially when we are stressed. Some things make our distress worse and these are things that we need to take care of today.

Let's return to the idea of HALT – hunger, anger, loneliness and tiredness. A stressful time is a difficult time, so you need as much energy as possible to cope with it. There is no point in trying to respond to stress if you are hungry, angry, lonely or tired – it's like going into the wrestling ring with your arms in plaster. Many of us remember times when a stressful event was made worse by one or more of these things. Now, in Step Eight, we must see these difficulties as opportunities.

In stressful times, remember Step Two. We must get our sleep and become rested. We need to be sober so we can be coherent. (It is a mistake to turn to alcohol – and anyway, the distraction of substance misuse disrupts our sleep.)

Our diet and exercise are not just sources of joy in themselves, but great restorative actions that will work in our favour.

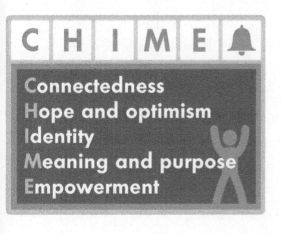

The same goes for human contact. CHIME tells us this is essential for recovery, and its loss is acutely felt at times of stress. The experience of lockdown during the COVID-19 pandemic made this even more apparent. Loneliness is a real and growing problem for many people, but especially for distressed people. An unrecognised effect of being lonely is the way it damages our response to other forms of stress.[lvi] Loneliness is not good for us. We need to challenge our aloneness in every way we can.

Step Eight of our whole new plan is about discovering the facts of our stress, but my patients have taught me also to understand the facts of distress. Let's do this, in order to consider our actions for recovery in a more particular way.

The facts of distress

When stress becomes more painful, more particular and more personally meaningful, then it's really distressing. Perhaps you have had a distressing major life event, or maybe a series of multiple, smaller events. The personal impact may make your distress difficult for others to understand. Sometimes it can even be difficult for you to identify. Sometimes you can feel it but cannot name it (Step Five). The distressed often ask themselves, 'What is happening to me?'

They ask themselves this same question over and over again, and when other emotions, like guilt, shame, rage and regret, rush to fill the mind's space, they still continue to question:

'Why am I letting this happen to me?'

'Am I responsible?'

'What does this say about me?'

Searching for answers to questions like this can be very tiring. A sense of injustice is very common after a distressful experience, especially after a trauma or a personal injury, and so it is understandable that people seek redress for the injustices done to them. Some people seek relief through the legal system, others seek it through the medical system, and many others find themselves on a meandering journey along both routes. The result is further distress that is partly determined by the route taken.

It doesn't need to be this way. The application of the law must see that justice is done. The practice of medicine should provide relief, but whichever avenue is taken, the options for those in distress need to be integrated. They need to provide more than a Hobson's choice between vindication or medication. Step Eight of our plan recognises that the restoration of health is the most important goal for the distressed, and that the appropriate journey is often a more therapeutic one.

Don't get me wrong. I have nothing against legal redress, nor am I opposed to prescribed medicine. However, there are times when neither of these is enough for those in distress. Recovery involves a rediscovery of meaning and a rebuilding of hope, and all of this needs time and love.

Many unexpected new understandings emerge through a therapeutic journey, including a whole new plan for living after distress, so when my patients talk about their experiences, they also help by articulating the facts of distress.

The first fact of distress

'Bad things happen to good people.'

This often-repeated truth is also one of the hardest things for distressed people to acknowledge and accept. For any distressed person, this is a tough reality to live with. After any blow, we wonder why we have been targeted in this way.

In Step Eight of our whole new plan for living we will stop blaming ourselves – blame is useless. Senseless, random wrongs happen to good people all the time. Those who experience violence or insult will still ask themselves what they did to cause the theft, the violence, the attack or the rape. This is understandable, but it's a mistake. There is no justifiable cause for an unjust act. In our distress, life is neither fair nor equal, and sadly we cannot avoid all the bad things that befall us.

Unfortunately, without someone else to blame, we resort to blaming ourselves. This self-blame is of no help either. On the occasions when an act of violence is carried out by someone else or because of something else, we must not share responsibility with the assailant. Pain and regret are heavy enough burdens for our shoulders, but responsibility for our violation is too much to carry. It is useless to feel guilt. Other people may lecture the 'victim' about taking 'responsibility' for their actions and 'owning' their experiences, but this is neither therapeutic nor just. Acceptance of trauma does not mean acceptance of guilt.

The second fact of distress

'You cannot change other people's behaviour; you can only change the way their behaviour makes you feel.'

Much of our response to stress, trauma and injury is amplified by wishing the trauma never happened. This is very distressing. We cannot wish for a better past; we can only work for a better present, and we must hope for a better future. In Step Eight of our whole new plan for living, we understand that we are not in charge of other people and we can't change their behaviour.

Responsibility for our own feelings is another matter. We can learn to think and feel in more compassionate, constructive ways, and especially to ourselves. This is true even after trauma. When acceptance and self-compassion take root, these restorative emotions act as balms to soothe our suffering. This idea of learning new ways of thinking after distress is at the centre of modern mental healthcare – and particularly of cognitive behavioural therapy. The way we think about things matters to our health. Changing our perspective can be life-saving. This is a therapeutic change we pursue in psychotherapy.

American psychiatrist Aaron T. Beck,[lvii] the father of CBT, reversed the standard hypothesis in mental health. Before Beck, it was believed that anxiety and depression came before our experiences. Beck suggested the reverse was the case – he proposed that our distress arose because of the way we think about our experience.

Subsequent evidence proved his hypothesis was correct: our negative views of ourselves, our future and our world cause us to become more depressed and anxious. In CBT, we set about learning some new ways of looking at ourselves, at the world and at our future in it. We learn new ways of thinking about ourselves and our lives.

This new learning is a key to our whole new plan for living. In order to be fully well, it is essential that we learn what we can and can't control.

The third fact of distress

'Survival is essential for success in life.'

When we witness someone in distress, we need to resist the temptation to tell them how to be well. 'Why don't you just get up, go out more, see your friends or get more exercise, go to a gym, do this, do that ...' The long road to recovery can become just one long harangue. In this book I have tried to avoid this trap, on the one hand giving guidance and on the other hand minimising instruction.

Over the years, I have tried to learn how to resist this temptation to advise and to avoid giving well-intentioned direction, but it takes courage to remain in the listening conversation, to hold back the impulse to suggest healthy things.

Wellness is not measured in terms of 'successful' behaviours. To paraphrase the American Jesuit Fr James Martin,[lviii] 'Our lives are not problems to be solved, they are mysteries to be lived.' We don't have to fix things all the time. We have to learn to live with many of them and to value that experience. For others, wealth, power or celebrity are measures of success, but those who have recovered see these things differently. They regard themselves as successful because they have survived and because they carry on. The measure of their success is their participation in their survival. Health and wellness are about living on, hoping to love another day.

At this point, we must address something else. If survival is success, then should we see death by suicide as a failure? I have been a witness to many a recovery, but I am not the author of recovery, and still less the judge of any. Survival is an essential component of our definition of wellbeing. Shocking as it is, the dead are gone from this world, and it remains for the living to recover in their loss. Those who die by suicide deserve our respect and our love, not our judgement (see Step Four). A life is valued for the way it is lived, not by the way it is ended. Every step of our whole new plan for living aims to reduce the number of people who die by suicide and to enable more people to survive their distress and carry on.

The fourth fact of distress

'Collaboration is essential. We need each other, just to get through.'

We are not alone. Whatever distress may be happening in your life right now, remember that this has happened before to someone else, and it will happen again to many other people. This acknowledgement is an act of fellowship and it can be very helpful. In Step Eight of our whole new plan for living we will seek out the fellowship of others who once experienced distress just as we do.

All over the country, fellowship groups meet to support one another through stress. One of the most difficult aspects of the COVID-19 lockdown was the way that it cut so many off from their fellowship and from support. From Men's Sheds to Aware, to Grow and to many others, people come and unite in support of one another through fellowship. Without necessarily articulating it, they lift one another just by their presence. They seem to say to one another, 'I am here for you, because I have been there before you, and I will be here for you again.' Fellowship is doubly rewarding: for sure it saves some lives, but it enriches many more.

It's important to maintain our connections in times of distress. Fellowship is a great way of remaining well. Whenever I talk to people who have gone backwards, who have relapsed or become distressed again, they tell me that they lost their fellowship. Relapse is no one's fault, and whether this isolation is a cause or an effect we will never know, but it is possible that they have lost the support of their group of friends. Step Eight of our whole new plan for living means remembering to maintain our support groups. Whether they are secular or religious, practical or playful, we must overcome the inner desire to isolate ourselves at times of distress and make a conscious decision not to stay away from those willing to understand us and our experiences.

Every step of our whole new plan for living reconnects us to our fellowship, wherever that happens to be and however this is possible. Connection is central to the eight dimensions of health. It is one of the five ways to wellness and it is the first word in CHIME – the features of successful recovery. After COVID-19 our reconnection may be virtual for a time, but even if we have lost our links, we will reconnect with them. So, as

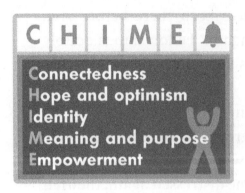

part of Step Eight, if your choir is your support, look forward to singing again. If dancing is your exercise, remember you will dance again. If your church is your fellowship, you will worship together again, and if you are a biker, you will ride again. Together we must find the people who can share our lives non-judgementally, and return to them.

The fifth fact of distress

'Everything passes – including our distress.'

This is a truth that has been told by the wise through the ages and it is still true today. Understanding the passing of things can be a great relief to the distressed. It may be very hard to believe at the time of greatest distress, but once it is grasped, the distressed discover that time is not the enemy; it is the bringer of great relief.

Sometimes when I see someone new in my room at St Patrick's Hospital, we take time to talk about this distress, and we listen to each other for a while. And sometimes later, we walk together along the hospital corridor outside my door. I like to stop and pause for a while, to take a look around at the eighteenth-century flagstones and admire the grandfather clock that stands in the corner.

'It looks like a very ordinary grandfather clock,' I like to say, 'but it's not. You see, it has a powerful history. This clock tells us a special lesson about our time and our recovery.'

My patient looks back and wonders what I could possibly be talking about. How could this clock be relevant to them? So, I like to explain.

'You see, this clock was bought in 1899 by Dr Richard Leaper. He was the medical director of St Patrick's Hospital from 1899 until 1944 and when he oversaw the modernisation of the hospital, he bought this, the hospital's first clock. For two hundred years before then there had been no clock in the hospital. Time had stopped since its foundation in 1745. Back then there was no reasonable expectation of recovery, and so there was no need for time. Those admitted to the hospital in the eighteenth and nineteenth centuries were confined to a place where there was little prospect for healthy life and where no one bothered to count the years. The world just stood still for these people. After all, what was the point in counting time? Those abandoned to the mental asylum had lost everything, including the right to a mentally healthy life, or anything that included time.'

In buying the clock, the good Dr Leaper made an important statement about hope: he acknowledged the value of time for himself, in the hope of restoring time for others. I like to imagine that he believed the distressed could recover in their time. By giving them back time, he was giving the distressed their rights and his timely help. We can recover ourselves in time. Without time there can be no recovery. Time is our opportunity and our hope. To go through distress – to triumph through it – it is necessary to embrace the mystery of time. Everything passes, even mental distress ... and all in good time.

Recovery

It's a Wonderful Life

Late on Christmas Eve in 2019, just as I was preparing to leave for the holidays, the phone in my office rang. I had finished my last day as the medical director of St Patrick's University Hospital, and I had no idea what was coming in 2020. I couldn't foresee the huge challenges ahead arising from the pandemic.

So, I picked up the phone. It was Sherry, our principal occupational therapist, and I supposed she was calling to wish me good luck in my retirement from my role as medical director. I thanked her and we chatted for a while about our years working together. Then she got to her subject.

'Maybe you could help us to make one last decision before you leave,' she said. 'We have a small dilemma ... it's about the Christmas movie. We decided to put it out to a vote. The aim was to let the people staying in the hospital for Christmas choose the film they would like to see on Christmas Day.'

'Great idea,' I said.

'Obviously most people are going home,' Sherry explained, 'but we thought it would be fun to have a real movie experience for those who are staying here, and we wanted to show something seasonal.'

'Sounds great,' I said. 'So what's the problem?'

'Well ... the thing is, most people voted to see the classic Jimmy Stewart movie *It's a Wonderful Life*. Actually, we wanted to show Will Ferrell's *Elf*, but less than half of the patients have asked for that.'

'So why don't you show both films?' I said.

'It's not that simple – you see, some of our department don't want to show *It's a Wonderful Life*. After all, it's a movie about a man who becomes acutely depressed and decides to take his own life.'

I paused for a moment before I replied, and then I just sighed.

'Sherry,' I said, 'do you know what I think? I think you should show that movie.'

'I was afraid you were going to say that,' she said.

So why am I telling you this story? It's because we are coming near the end of our whole new plan for living and I want to finish by saying some things about resilience and recovery. It's time for us to bring our whole new plan to its hopeful conclusion.

So far, I have shared with you what I have learned over the years about health and wellness, and about stress and distress. We have taken eight steps together but now it's time to talk about more sustaining things. All along I have been encouraging you to make a conscious blueprint of a plan for your wellbeing. Your whole new plan for living could be a set of fresh insights and changed behaviours, ones that you will put to good use for your life. But be sure of this: I have not been telling you how to live your life. All I am saying is that each of us can make a whole new plan for a better life.

Obviously, your plan is for yourself, but that does not make it selfish. There is a difference. A whole new plan for living is your blueprint of what French philosopher Michel Foucault[lix] termed the 'technologies of the self' or what I prefer to call 'the therapy of the self'. This is a process of learning to live well again and continuing to live better by loving yourself more. After all that has happened during the Covid-19 pandemic, surely we need to take better care of ourselves, and to prioritise our health so that we are able to take care of each other and our world. Our whole new plan for living is becoming more urgent every day. In making our plan, we began by raising awareness of our needs, and with each step we went a little further. Now we are translating our awareness into action for our wellbeing.

Our health issues are complex and challenging, and this is especially true when it comes to our mental health, but I hope by now you agree that simply talking about anxiety, depression and even suicide is not dangerous. But talking is not enough. Our mobilisation for action begins with this conversation about our mental health, so it is truly urgent. In my view, talking about these things has never hurt anyone. It is the inability to talk about our thoughts and our feelings that hurts more people every day.

So, why am I going on about this classic movie, *It's a Wonderful Life*? Obviously, it's a wonderful movie, but it's neither a therapy nor a hazard for our health. My point is this: the film by Frank Capra expresses almost everything that I believe in. It's a darkly modern fairytale that reminds us of our human potential for despair or for renewal, and it reminds us that we are made resilient by our human connectedness, by our relationships with ourselves and by our collaboration with others.

Wherever you look, at politics and sport, in art and cinema, in drama and poetry, you will find that this humane point is being reiterated. It is a life-and-death message. Stress and distress are genuine parts of our everyday existence. Jimmy Stewart's George Bailey may have had 'a wonderful life', but the point of the story is that even he reached his breakdown point. As we have said, a breakdown can happen to anyone. His rediscovery of his connectedness helps him recover, and our whole new plan (and each of its steps) is a similar route for our health and our wellness.

Now it's time to consider how Step Eight of our whole new plan for living can help us to recover and to become more resilient before we are also at that edge. How can we plan to have a wonderful life?

CHIME – the features of recovery

Throughout this book I have been referring to 'CHIME', the features of recovery. Recovery is the restoration of health and wellness after a setback. Resilience is the ability to bounce back from each new distress. Every recovery is different. Resilience requires the capacity to adapt to stress and to reframe our distress in positive ways. This elastic ability varies across people and over time. Recent research in mental health found that a set of human characteristics summarised by the acronym CHIME accurately describe the typical features of recovery. We have touched on each of these throughout this book. So now let's recap on these characteristics and go into each one in more detail.

Connectedness

Connectedness is vital for recovery. An enduring sense of disconnect is common in many illnesses, but this is characteristic of mental distress and disorder. There are times when we all need to withdraw from others, but restoring our connection is an essential action

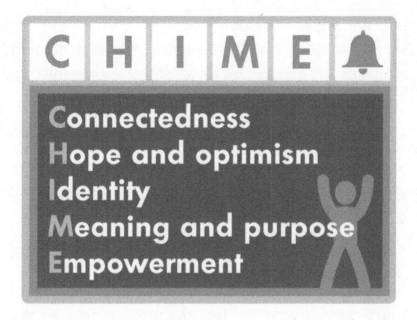

C H I M E

Connectedness
Hope and optimism
Identity
Meaning and purpose
Empowerment

practically and psychologically for recovery, and deep down, we know this is true. There are bound to be times when we need to be alone, but prolonged isolation is invariably bad for us. Captives and prisoners know this well. They know it's very painful to be cut off from others. This explains why we visit the sick and why we 'make that call'. Being alone, feeling alone, is a form of jeopardy. We rediscovered this during the pandemic, when COVID-19 prevented us from visiting our cocooned relatives, our sick and elderly: we felt this distress and doubtless so did they. We grieved heavily for the loss of our connections.

So, in Step Eight of our whole new plan for living we will restore our connections. This may not be an easy part of our whole new plan but it's a vital one. Care is better when it is connected – by joining things up we become coherent. These fragile connections are both within us and between us. Recovery means reconnecting and being made whole again by these links.

Hope and optimism

No recovery is possible without hope. Any valid, effective therapy depends on this resource. Hope brings with it the prospect of relief.

Optimism sustains our ability to travel towards recovery more hopefully. Without hope, there can be no journey to health, and sadly no destination other than the one we fear the most. It follows that any therapeutic system dedicated to recovery must encourage optimism and hope. In Step Eight of our whole new plan for living we will be sustained by that same hope and optimism.

Identity

Individual recovery requires recognition of our diverse identity, the discovery of who we are. We acknowledged this in Step Six. Every person seeking recovery needs and deserves this unique respect. Stigma and dismissal can have no place in a humane and therapeutic healthcare system. Many disadvantaged groups such as the wheelchair-bound, the disabled, and those marginalised by prejudice because of their race or orientation, have had to fight long and hard for this recognition of their identity. Once an identity is lost, the awareness of an individual is lost. And once the recognition of the individual is lost, the awareness of their needs and their rights is also gone. This search for identity continues throughout the recovery journey, and so back in Step Six we reiterated the mantra of many service users: 'let there be nothing about me that is without me'. Respect for each identity in recovery is a human rights value. Without this respect, health services risk neglecting their patients' rights as well as failing to meet their needs. Rediscovery of personal identity becomes a defining characteristic of a recovery-based service. This discovery in an individual is akin to a personal awakening and it is a joy to witness.

Recovering our identity creates respect. Seen in this way, a woman with diabetes is not 'a diabetic' – she is someone with an endocrine problem. A man with schizophrenia is not a 'schizophrenic' – he is someone with a mental health difficulty. And so each person with a challenge becomes a human being with their own identity, their own rights and their own new plan for living.

Meaning and purpose

A life without meaning would be distressing and, even if such a life were to emerge, it would not be sustained. In *Man's Search for Meaning*, Viktor Frankl's 1946 autobiography,[ix] he describes his terrible experience of captivity in Nazi concentration camps during the Second World War, and he proposes that 'meaning' is life-saving for us.

A meaningful life comes in many different guises. It can come from a job or a project, a book you want to write, a person you want to be with, a love you want to cherish, or a child you want to see grow. The important thing is that you see this pursuit as worth living for and that makes your life sustainable. With meaning we come to believe that our life is worth recovering for.

In clinical practice, we place great value on meaningful relationships. We see them as protective, so when we have that recurring conversation about the desire for life or death, the listening conversation when we ask about thoughts of suicide, we believe the presence of a protective relationship can make all the difference. I asked one patient of mine:

'So, tell me, have you ever felt despair?'

My patient answered this by saying, 'Yes, of course, I feel despair.'

'And would you do it?'

'Do what?' he replied.

'Would you take your own life?'

'Never,' he insisted.

'And why is that? What stops you from ending your life?' I asked.

'My children, my love for my wife, my thinking of the pain they would feel if I succumbed to this awful moment.'

Whether a psychiatrist should be reassured by this response from his patient is debatable. The evidence after fifty years of research[lxi] is that attempts to stratify risk are not reliable. Assessment of risk is an unsatisfactory practice, but it is still an essential part of today's mental healthcare. A meaningful relationship can save a life and is protective, at least for a time, and so we accept this reassurance and we carry on, both looking for recovery. We recognise that the alternative – a life without meaning – is a life in real danger.

Empowerment

Recovery requires engagement and the empowerment of the distressed person. To help someone recover, we – the families and neighbours, the carers and health services – must empower others to recover. This is not the same thing as nagging them. We cannot pressurise or dupe people into getting well. Recovery is an integral process and an authentic one. The rights and the responsibilities of each person are at its heart, so we need to give someone the power to get well. That is why an ethical service must respect the autonomy of each service user. We try to be of benefit, and so we must defend our patients' autonomy. The route to recovery is a just route and not an end.

An effective plan is more likely to be one that is sustained. No matter how good a plan looks on paper, it is useless unless it empowers someone to continue with their new plan for living, whether this means medication, therapy, lifestyle change, or all three. In Step Eight of our whole new plan for living, recovery is about restoring our power to do whatever works for us.

Kindness

How can we empower recovery and make things CHIME? One answer is through greater kindness. Our whole new plan for living is a strategic one, moving us towards a) the recognition of our own value as human beings and b) the acceptance of wellness as the only success worth having. These two goals will be impossible without greater kindness. We learned this in Step Four. Relationships built on anger are bound to fail because they begin without genuine mutual regard. On the other hand, a relationship built on kindness begins with compassion for yourself, and this can grow. Love for others starts with our kindness to ourselves.

When it comes to the traditional approach to health, we have been looking at things from the wrong end of the telescope, by looking at disease rather than wellness. In times of distress and frustration, the pain we feel is best mitigated by taking greater care of ourselves. Loving yourself means being kinder to yourself. Without kindness to ourselves, it is difficult to be well. This compassion in our inner lives can transform our experience of everyday life. Our whole new plan for living is about finding within us a genuine sense of warmth that sustains us. In deep distress, this place of self-care is unsustainable without kindness. Discovering this seed of love, however small, is empowering.

Each of us has within us an inner self that is trying to survive. Our inner self could be the person we really are and the source of the person we would like to become. Imagine your inner self as the child you once were. This is not some romantic idea. It is an invaluable discovery in our new plan for living, and so we will try to be kinder to our inner self. This kindness is an empowering investment. It means healing the person we once were and becoming the person we could be.

Imagine how good life could be if we were all more kind. During the COVID-19 crisis many people found new ways to be kind. The simplest of kindnesses could yield the warmest responses from others. Our new plan is about learning to leave behind the harshest experiences of our past in order to create a kinder experience of the present. Loving yourself means undoing all the harsh judgements you have of yourself and of everyone else (see Step Three, page 71). The effect will be the undoing of your distress, and this will be life-changing. Harsh judgement only begets harsh judgement, and kindness begets kindness. In our whole new plan for living, we will work towards a kinder experience of ourselves by making our lives a kinder experience for others. In this way Step Eight will empower us to recovery and make us more resilient than before.

Step Nine

Tools for Your Whole New Plan

Back at the start of this journey, we agreed to begin our whole new plan for living simply with a blank page and a pencil. We started with an open mind and a hopeful heart, noting the features of our wellbeing, the eight dimensions of good health and the five ways to wellness. Then we took some time to look at the realities of everyday life and to consider some common sources of our difficulty including burnout and other mental health difficulties.

Next, we looked at our identity. This is the part of the exercise that made our whole new plan unique. The problems we experience may be similar in some respects and many of them are shared, but in other ways our challenges are singular and unique because each of us is individual. Our particular problems reflect the life we have; they are not indicative of who we are. Neither are they descriptors of our identity as persons. Whether our problems are episodic or continuing, singular or complex, they are not what we are about. Our problems define our experience, not our identity.

So now our whole new plan is nearly ready. That sheet of paper you started with is no longer blank, but there is more to be done. Our work is not over. It's time for your plan to become a uniquely personal and special agenda, something tangible in the context of your life. In making this plan for yourself you have probably been asking yourself some other questions, like, 'How can I really adopt the five ways to wellness?' 'What greater priority can I give to my health?' 'What can I do to sustain any of this?' This questioning is good – it will make your plan grow and become more relevant, by making it more particular to yourself. This is a time for perseverance.

Throughout the making of our whole new plan for living I have encouraged you to become more aware of the collective and environmental measures necessary for our better health, since the biggest health benefits arise from public things that we all share. By contrast to population health, our individual progress towards a better life is made in much smaller steps, each pieced together more patiently. We must not be discouraged by this small progress. Our new personal plan attends to our life, whereas public health initiatives reflect the general population need. Our daily advance is on a smaller scale, and rightly so. Still, our greater public health awareness is not utopian; for our better health we must care about our environment, about peace, about justice and about our shared prosperity. So remember, the benefits of almost any individual steps are small when compared to those sustained by better policy in public health and mental health. The COVID-19 pandemic has taught us that collective measures are essential, since they empower us as individuals to recover.

Working on the detail of your whole new plan: what tools will you need?

Your new plan is already at an advanced stage. Maybe you have been building it up slowly – but now is the time to be more focused. We know what the goal is, and now we need to finalise a route map towards that goal. We have agreed that our goal is 'wellness' and we have agreed a broad definition of that concept, so what practical tips do we need at this stage? What 'skills' do we require to put all this planning finally into action for today and every day? There are four tips I often recommend:

1. Routine and structure

2. Reframing

3. Recovery

4. Resilience

Let's go into each one in more detail.

Routine and structure

Start the day as you finish it, take time to have a moment of reflection. Take notice of the good progress you have already made and do this each day. Let your worst results go by the wayside. Remember, the negative is much more adhesive than the positive. Try to make your positive progress stick and then be grateful for it.

Keep a diary and learn to enjoy the ebb and flow of your daily campaign as it takes you along its way. Never forget that you're on the road to your discovery of a better life, and it will come. There will be a time when you will sing and dance, and laugh and play, and do this all again and again.

Now draw yourself into your plan. Go as far as possible to place yourself on the paper, even on a graph where the horizontal axis is time and the vertical axis is health. Make a map of your progress. In any week, month or year, watch yourself take more steps, rising higher and higher on the health axis, as you continue to apply each step of your new plan for living. And when you fall back (as at times we all do), don't worry. Now you are armed with your whole new plan for living, you can always restart it, to succeed and to live well again.

Managing our anxiety – the three 'Rs'

By taking Step Nine of your whole new plan you will be using as many tools for wellness as you can find. Learning to make your new plan for living much more effective means re-learning the three 'Rs'. These are not Reading, Writing and Arithmetic, but the three 'Rs' of anxiety management: reframing, recovery and resilience. We will consider each of these briefly but before we do there are some things we must remember about our anxiety.

Anxiety is a normal response to our stress, but panic is not helpful or mindful (especially in the middle of a global pandemic). To paraphrase our then taoiseach, Leo Varadkar, during his COVID-19 statement back in March 2020, 'Anxiety also spreads like a virus.' So, try to remember the facts of stress and distress. Panic is pointless, and so to survive this current health crisis (or any other) and come out of it in better shape, we must take better care of ourselves and of each other.

That's what your plan is all about. Now let's look into the three 'Rs' of anxiety management in more detail.

Reframing

Reframing is a basic skill of anxiety management and is an important method of healing. It means to refocus your attention and to respond to stress and distress more functionally. We can start by understanding where our fears come from and then we reframe that understanding in a more compassionate way.

We already know that all our worst fears relate to three core agendas: anxiety for ourselves, for our future and for our world. This cognitive triad described by Aaron T. Beck (see also page 90) is a summary of the core concerns of every human being, but even still these fears are subjective, and so they can be changed: they can be 'reframed'. At times of stress we all fear for our own safety, our future, and the survival of our environment. Our environmental anxiety includes fears for our personal environment – our shared home and community – as well as the wider one.

Instead of being frightened by these three agendas, we could focus and revalue them.[lxii] Values are things that we hold very dear. They uplift us, whereas anxieties drain us. In our whole new plan for living we will continue by revaluing our lives, our future and our world, and we will plan to take better care of all of these.

This renewed awareness of our values and concerns empowers us. By reframing our anxieties into values, we can move our anxiety into a better, more positive, more active space. With this awareness, we can make better plans to defend the things we care about most. So in your whole new plan let's try to practise some 'reframing'. Write down your anxieties. Now reframe them as values, as positives and as plans. Suppose you are worried about your job or your relationship with your family. Think instead about how you value your job, how you love your partner, and how you care for your family. What was once a list of worries can be transformed into a description of your values and an agenda of your opportunities. Reframing moves your anxiety along constructive avenues towards planned actions and these become the antidote to your anxiety.

Reframing our anxiety about the COVID-19 pandemic is possible by replacing our worries with more positive values. This means putting a greater value on our future, and a greater value on our world. From now on our agendas of distress could become our initiatives for commitment. These worries are things we care deeply about, not just fears we panic about. Our areas of concern could be transformed in our whole new plan into constructive responses for our whole new life. Awareness of our values first steadies us, then it mobilises us to coherent action. A healthy cycle of reframing our worries into more positive values and constructive action goes as follows:

anxieties > values > awareness > action

Recovery

Step Nine of our whole new plan means applying effective tools to make recovery happen. For recovery after COVID-19, or after any calamity, we need to believe in the potential of our lives. This belief is evidence-based. It is a commitment to our capacity as a species. It says that we will not be overcome. We can redefine what we mean by being well, despite the rising tide of zoonoses (see page 41) and many other environmental challenges (like global warming and loss of habitat) arising in the modern world. Belief in our recovery[lxiii] is essential for our survival. It is a tool for success. Without this belief our anxiety goes out of control and we are left in a state of panic.

We can be the authors of recovery. These are stressful times, but there will be more stresses to come. Educating ourselves now to the fullest awareness of our environmental hazards is mindful. It is essential. Our era has been called 'the age of anxiety' and with good reason. The world is warming, species and habitats are declining, wars are constant, and millions of people are being forced into migration and modern-day slavery. Surely an anxiety response is appropriate in the face of all this.

To find a whole new plan for living, we need to believe in our capacity to overcome these challenges. Recovery is a process, not a conclusion. We know what this process will involve. Recovery happens when we invest in things that CHIME, an acronym which we are well accustomed to at this stage of our whole new plan. So recovery is enabled by connecting people with hope, respecting their identity, accepting their meaning and empowering them to meet their goals. This leadership is a human necessity at any time but an urgent one at this stressful time. If we believe in recovery, we will unite around these recovery principles. Engagement in recovery will be transformative. It could redefine the whole understanding of our lives.

Resilience

Back in Step Three, we talked about letting things go, about understanding the folly of tenacity in every circumstance. So why am I encouraging you now to be resilient? Why not let our new plan go when the going gets tough? Is there any need for tenacity when keeping to a whole new plan? How can we resolve this apparent contradiction and what does this tell us about the possibility of success of our whole new plan for living?

Lest there be any confusion, allow me to explain.

Tenacity is a mistake when it means holding on to ideas and emotions that are destructive to our health, like bewilderment or anger. But resilience is valuable because it is the ability to bounce back and to adapt to challenges with new ways of being well. The tenacious run the risk of being ground down by life, whereas the resilient regrow and refresh their world. That's the difference. Our whole new plan must be a new, resilient plan, not an old, failed plan that we adhered to with tenacity. Now in Step Nine it is time to harness our resilience. This is the source of the ability to bounce back after a crisis.[lxiv] After COVID-19 we need to be resilient. Our world will not recover as a collection of weakened nations, a network of peoples less prepared for the next crisis, too weakened to appreciate the next opportunity. We can be resilient.

Resilience is not a single characteristic. It is the summation of many facets of our life and of our experience. Each of us becomes more resilient when we restore the domains that make us elastic and resourceful. By making our whole new plan, we will redefine our understanding of recovery. We know from research what generates resilience in young people and we know that these same things increase resilience in us. We can build our resilience by enhancing six domains:

1. Education

2. Security

3. Social competency

4. Friendships

5. Talents and interests

6. Positive values

All of these are connected domains and they are humane. They are not absolute, and they can always be replenished. Investing in these for the sake of our life resonates with the five ways to wellness and coincides with the eight domains of health. So, in Step Nine of our whole new plan for living, let's think of opportunities to enlarge these 'resilience domains'. Ask yourself how you can grow these potential sources of your elastic energy – your bounce-back-ability. Replenish these drivers of your recovery by rebuilding these things and, by making them your priority, you will be making the next step of your whole new plan.

Ten tools to help you manage your anxiety and carry on with life

Reframing, recovering and being resilient are somewhat abstract ways of describing your whole new plan for living. Perhaps a more concrete and practical expression of these ideas is necessary. Let me finish Step Nine of our whole new plan for living with another, very practical list of tools which I hope you will find helpful. These ten practical steps can be applied to any crisis. Indeed, they could become parts of your whole new plan for living.

1. Respect yourself.

2. Consider sound advice and take it. Learn to manage your consumption of information to avoid additional stress and instead be led by reliable scientific evidence, not by panic or fear.

3. Be quiet for some part of each day, by being more mindful, or by meditating, or just by limiting your exposure to the twenty-four-hour news cycle.

4. Sleep and eat as well as you can and take exercise every day, wherever you are.

5. Reframe your worries – think of them as your values rather than your fears.

6. Believe in your recovery – support the things that make your recovery possible.

7. Practise hope – not as a vague or unimaginable concept but as an essential essence for life.

8. Stay connected with those you love, limit your use of social media, especially anything hostile

or toxic, write letters to yourself about how
you're progressing with your whole new plan.

9. Discover (recover) the meaning of your life
    (whatever that is) and focus on it – whatever
    it is.

10. Grow your resilient domains – your education,
    your talents and interests, your friendships
    and your positive values.

Taken together, this phase of your whole new plan
makes common sense. It makes individual sense and it
makes societal sense. It even makes economic sense. A
healthier you will be a happier, more connected, more
productive you. Your individual recovery, your new
life, will benefit the economy and your community.
Your value to the economy is not only monetary, nor is
it short-term. Your whole new plan for living will be a
better plan if it incorporates a whole-of-health view of
living economics. Your plan could make your country
a better place, a more attractive place, a happier
place in which to live and be well, and that would
make economic sense. Step Nine of your whole new
plan encourages you to take the tools of reframing,
resilience and recovery, to help you to get to a better
place, so that together we can make this a better place
to live, work and love.

What to do when Balance is Lost

So far we have described aspects of our health, wellness and identity in general as part of the formation of a whole new plan. Now it's time to consider some specific problems that you may be facing right now or that you may face in the future. In Step Ten we will discuss some common mental health difficulties that could arise. These are universal issues, but they may need to be addressed by you or by someone you care about in order to make further progress. Some of these issues may not be relevant to your plan for wellness but let's take the time to consider them, just the same.

Clinical depression

Depression is the largest single cause of disability in the Western world.[lxv] It is also the greatest contributor to the tragedy of completed suicide. Moderate to severe depression is a health emergency that demands an urgent response, but in many countries this response is delayed and inadequate. This is more than disappointing, since clinical depression is actually a very treatable disorder. Most people with depression make a full recovery when they are offered the right treatment.

Untreated depression remains very common in the community, and unfortunately this depression frequently co-exists with other mental health problems, most commonly anxiety disorder. One in five of us will have a depressive illness at some stage in our lives.[lxvi] The onset is typically early in adult life; three-quarters of these mental health problems commence before the age of twenty-five.

Treatment for depression may not be straightforward – there is a huge amount of trial and error in the treatment process. Antidepressants work for some people, but they are not universally effective. It is as if an antidepressant has to fit the person – only a third of my patients respond to the first antidepressant prescribed, so, many continue trying a second or even a third drug before finding the right one. Modern evidence-based algorithms have helped to standardise this care, but the pursuit of an efficacious care package for depression can be a long one. Any drug treatment will be more successful when combined with psychological treatments. This more effective therapeutic treatment combination is sometimes called the 'care plan'.

The extended journey to wellness for some people with moderate to severe clinical depression comes on top of other delays accessing mental healthcare. All of these can be very frustrating. The burden of delay bears heavily on both patients and their loved ones, requiring some to be possessed of almost monastic patience. Enduring a prolonged experience of depression adds to the fear of future relapses. It is hardly surprising that many people decide to maintain their medication. Some find, through a process of trial and error, that the best way for them to stay well is to continue doing the things that got them well in the first place.

There is truth in this. Continuity of care is important. The resolution of depression is not just about getting well, it is about staying well. Nearly 50 per cent of people with a major depressive illness relapse within their lifetime, and 80 per cent of those who experience a second illness will relapse yet again.[lxvii]

Therefore, the decision to remain on an effective antidepressant is an important option for a growing number of women and men. These people recognise their need to do whatever works for them in their effort to stay well. They are entitled to live a mentally healthy life and so they should not be shamed. People who take antidepressants and remain well on them are not drug abusers. They are people in recovery. Sticking to an effective treatment could be part of their whole new plan for living, a choice made by many people with a right to live a mentally healthy life.

Prescribing antidepressant medications

According to recent Irish data,[lxviii] 'the number of patients prescribed antidepressants through publicly funded drug schemes increased by 18 per cent between 2012 and 2017. The dosages being prescribed during the same period increased by 28 per cent in per capita terms. Similar findings exist around the globe – and especially in the world's richest nations: more antidepressants are being prescribed than ever before. So why is this happening?

Examining the differences in prescribing rates across many regions of Ireland tells us something about the reasons for the growing use of these antidepressants. There is one correlation that explains things more than any other. The rising use of antidepressants is linked to the lack of availability of any alternatives in certain regions. The alternatives to medication, such as psychotherapeutic services, are least available where prescribing is greatest. Consequently, too little help is being offered to those in most need of help. If we really want to limit prescribing antidepressants, we need to provide a much fuller range of psychotherapeutic treatments fit for the twenty-first century. But when alternatives are scarce, higher volumes of prescriptions are the inevitable result.

So, what should we say about the rising amount of antidepressants being prescribed to increasing numbers of people? Would a healthier society be less depressed? In our whole new plan for living we will need to educate ourselves about the reality of clinical depression – a problem that is part of the human experience of suffering, and which is no less of an illness than heart disease or cancer – and stop shaming those who take antidepressants and cease from chastising those who achieve a recovery on them. With recovery, people start to live and work and love again. Antidepressants could be a part of a plan for living, but a whole new plan would include better prevention of illness and, when necessary, more freely available psychological treatments. We could and should make therapeutic care planning available to everyone and we should remove any vestige of shame from such treatment.

Talking to someone with depression:
listening conversation

People experience depression in different ways: some seem to be their usual selves, while others are unable to continue their normal routine. Depression can cause people to feel unbearable pain or deadening numbness.

It can impair their ability to think, speak and feel connected to others.

Our difficulties talking about this subject are indicative of other anxieties. Many of us are afraid of a conversation with someone who is depressed. Others are exhausted by it, tired of saying the wrong thing, fearing it will do more harm than good. For all our national reputation for the 'gift of the gab' we have a deep-rooted belief that 'least said, soonest mended'. This cultural attitude was parodied by the late Seamus Heaney in his poem 'Whatever You Say, Say Nothing'. Added to all this is the persistent effect of our oldest enemy: stigma. We are in too much denial to speak to each other about our deepest need – the need to be supported when we are in despair. The worst fear of all is the fear of being a burden to others.

There may be better ways to think about depression and many other ways to talk about it. Sometimes, however, talking is not what is needed. Sometimes, we just need to listen and to do this actively. I call this 'listening conversation' (see also page 7), but Carl Rogers called it 'active listening'.[lxix] It is fair to say that 'active listening' is different from our usual sort of chat. It is a kinder, more thoughtful and more considerate kind of exchange. Listening conversation is about hearing others' distress and still being there, holding each other and holding on, at least for a time. Step Ten of our whole new plan is about creating an environment where we listen and where we hear each other in more helpful ways.

So how should we talk to someone with depression? It helps to think about who the person is, rather than worrying about what we ought to say. When we consider the experience of another person in distress, we become less preoccupied with our own speech. Listening conversation can help us to do this and to recover our lost empathy. We begin to hear the depressed person inviting us to 'walk in their shoes'. The conversation becomes less of an interrogation and more about the restoration of a relationship. Listening conversation forms a bridge that connects us to others at different stages of their journey. These conversations happen between the young and old, between women and men, between employers and colleagues, between neighbours and friends. These listening conversations involve all of us.

No one is saying this communication is going to be easy, and there will be no perfect opportunity. Awareness of each other's identity (discussed in Step Six) helps as well. Teens and young adults may be more at ease talking about their mental health with a trusted adult rather than directly to their parents. Parents may not feel comfortable talking to their children about their own or other family members' mental health. Adults may find it difficult to talk to their elderly parents about their mental health or their possible early dementia. In each situation, a trusted adult, a friend or a mentor could help to make the engagement and the conversation easier.

Remember that listening conversation is not about giving advice. However eager you may be to do this, know that advice-giving is best avoided. This may seem contradictory now, when we have spent the past nine steps giving each other nothing but good advice, but know this: telling someone to go for a walk or join a gym or have a nice warm bath is not going to help the person with the mental health difficulty. If someone doesn't want to talk, then a listening conversation means hearing that and accepting the response, while always leaving the option open for the other person to talk later. Instead of persisting in trying to get someone to talk, try sending a supportive text, offering to pop round, or simply asking how you can be supportive or helpful.

At times you may feel that you have got it wrong when you have been trying to be supportive, but don't reproach yourself. Your guilt only makes your connection more difficult. Try taking small steps and bring all things into balance. Speak gently. Listen, even in silence. If you don't feel that you are making a difference, look for an alternative approach. Practise kindness and, most importantly, don't feel the need to offer solutions.

You cannot fake empathy. It's not helpful to say to someone, 'I know exactly how you feel.' In reality it's unlikely that you do. And don't feel that you must have all the answers. Listening conversation isn't judgemental; it's mindful. It's about being there, reaching out and, most of all, holding on.

So, I hear you ask, will this approach be effective? Yes, it could be. The best evidence is that families and friends with more open communication are more supportive. In Step Ten of our whole new plan for living we will practise this listening conversation. Too many people continue to experience their mental distress without ever being able to have this conversation at all.

Panic anxiety

Everyone gets anxious from time to time, and in modern life this is perfectly understandable. In Step Eight, we considered the difference between stress and distress in detail but for now it's sufficient to say that anxiety is an appropriate response to the events of our world. Some life circumstances produce more anxiety than others. The recent COVID-19 pandemic is a good example of this: it has created a whole new level of fear and anxiety in many more people.

Whether you are at work or at home, in more confined spaces or in the open, feeling anxious is inevitable at times of stress. There are occasions where it may even be helpful to feel anxious. Anxiety readies us. It is a response to stress that enables us to prepare for a fight and, if necessary, to take flight. Without anxiety, we would have no early-warning system and we would all be defenceless.

Experiencing panic anxiety is a different matter. Panic is distressing and panic attacks are crescendos of extreme anxiety arising from a sudden, unexpected outpouring of adrenalin and noradrenalin (the brain form of adrenalin) that floods the body and the brain. Anyone who has experienced such an attack even once will find it hard to forget. A panic attack is a truly terrifying form of distress. The list of symptoms experienced is very long, but an attack may include any or all of the following:

* Palpitations (accelerated heartbeat)

* Sweating

* Trembling and shaking

* Pins and needles

* Hot flushes and cold chills

* Shortness of breath

* Choking or smothering

* Chest pains

* Nausea or abdominal pain

* Dizziness or faintness

Most people having a panic attack fear that they are losing control. They may even believe that they are going 'crazy'. Others fear their world is becoming entirely unreal. At their worst, panic attacks make people feel they are about to die. This experience can last for as little as ten minutes, or as long as several hours.

Although panic attacks are very common, it is not helpful to dismiss these experiences as 'normal' parts of daily life – no one should have to learn to live with such distressing events. Panic attacks are disabling phenomena, but they are also highly treatable. Mindfulness, cognitive behavioural therapy and some medications including antidepressants (known as serotonin re-uptake inhibitors) have all been shown to be effective. In Step Ten of our whole new plan for living we will need to respond to our anxiety differently. This means continuing with changes to our lifestyle and to our self-care that characterise our plan (see Steps Two and Three), since by doing this we will undo what one of my patients calls 'the dynamics of panic'. This is a practical approach to panic which gives us the answer to panic, and this is greater peace.

Alcohol use and misuse

Alcohol misuse is a common, clandestine problem. Alcohol has been described as our 'favourite drug', but many of us shrink from acknowledging our personal alcohol reality. These are the facts.

Alcohol use increases risks to our health for two reasons – firstly, because of the amount we consume and, secondly, because of the pattern of our consumption.

In English-speaking countries we tend towards a 'binge pattern' of alcohol misuse. This is a pattern in which we drink intermittently, but when we do drink, we really go for it – we drink to get drunk. In Ireland, we consume the equivalent of one bottle of spirits per adult, per week. Every night in Ireland at least 1,500 acute hospital beds (13 per cent of our national resource) are occupied as a direct result of alcohol misuse.[lxx]

But it is the cultural significance of our alcohol misuse that is most telling. When I was young, we were told that alcohol was 'good' for us. We grew up with this slogan, and it was repeated often, like a mantra. At some level back then, we believed that alcohol wasn't harmful to us and that it might even be healthy to drink it.

Even now our marketing of alcohol is more powerful and more manipulative than some are prepared to acknowledge. The dominance of alcohol advertising in sport is one clear example of this. In this way the manufacturers have associated alcohol use with fitness, health and satisfaction, just as the makers of cigarettes associated their consumption with power, charm and sex appeal.

The reality is very different. Alcohol does not increase our joy; it operates chemically by decreasing our inhibition. It is a factor in many diseases, disorders and injuries. It also contributes to many of our social problems and is a cause of many cancers,[lxxi] such as cancers of the mouth, the oesophagus, the larynx and the breast. It also damages vital organs, such as the brain, the liver and the pancreas.

Alcohol misuse in pregnancy leads to foetal growth retardation, learning disabilities and foetal alcohol syndrome. Alcohol exacerbates common medical conditions, such as raised blood pressure, gastritis, diabetes and stroke, but it also aggravates every kind of mental health problem known, including dementia. Its use is associated with many deaths through road-traffic collisions, pedestrian injuries, falls and injuries at work. In 2018 the authoritative medical journal *The Lancet* concluded that 'no level of alcohol consumption improves your health'.[lxxii]

The bottom line is that alcohol is not good for us and it never was. The debate about our alcohol use has become unbalanced. The majority of the tools for alcohol promotion are in the hands of the drinks industry but all the responsibility for its misuse falls on the shoulders of individuals, families and taxpayers. In Ireland we have a laissez-faire attitude to the promotion of alcohol but if we approached our other health and safety issues with the same attitude, we would have little regulation anywhere. When it comes to a healthy lifestyle, our attitude to alcohol is not liberal. It is harmful.

It's not all bad news. Recently in Scotland and Ireland a form of 'minimum pricing' legislation has been introduced, to prevent strong alcohol being sold at very cheap prices. You can tell this is a good idea because the drinks industry fought very hard to prevent it. Now, the world waits to see if these reforms will work to reduce misuse and misery related to alcohol. In the meantime, in Step Ten of our whole new plan for living, we will need to be better informed about our alcohol use. We will need to make better decisions around our favourite drug.

Alcohol dependency

Sometimes my patients say to me, 'I do like a drink, but I am not an alcoholic.' I'm sure someone has said this to you at some point – maybe you've even said it yourself. Whenever I hear this denial, it always makes me think. It's worth pondering the language we use to describe our use of alcohol.

What do people really mean when they say things

like: 'I am not a drinker … I just like the occasional glass of wine' or 'I don't actually drink … except at weddings and parties'? Could it be that we are unable to accurately acknowledge our use of alcohol, and we find it even harder to acknowledge the damage our use of alcohol is causing to our health and wellbeing?

No one wants to be labelled an alcoholic, and in practice this term is of very little use in my clinic. I rarely use it. What I'm interested in knowing, and what any doctor wants to know, is whether someone's use of alcohol has become hazardous, harmful or even dependent. In Step Ten of our whole new plan we want to know more about our alcohol use, and this will help us to sustain our whole new way of living. Step Ten means making better choices about our drinking.

Some people drink large amounts of alcohol each and every day and this drinking may be described as hazardous. Many others drink alcohol intermittently, but when they do, they drink until they are drunk. These are the binge drinkers and they are the largest single group of problem drinkers seen in our clinical practice. These people drink in a way which is harmful to them, and they keep returning to it even though their alcohol use is clearly damaging their physical or mental health. Lastly, there are some people who drink in a persistent, dependent and addicted way. These people find it very difficult to stop drinking even though it is obvious to everyone that alcohol is bad for their health and for the lives of those around them. These three patterns indicate three distinctive behaviours of alcohol misuse. So, in Step Ten of our whole new plan for living it is time to know more about our alcohol use. It's time to take the AUDIT test – the Alcohol Use Disorders Identification Test.

The AUDIT test

It's helpful to describe our alcohol use more accurately and to recognise whether it is hazardous, harmful or dependent. A simple way to do this is to take the Alcohol Use Disorders Identification Test (AUDIT).[lxxiii] This is a valid and reliable test. It is available to anyone, free of charge and readily accessed on the internet. The AUDIT's greatest value is in its use as a self-report measure. With the AUDIT there are no winners and no losers. All we need is to be honest with ourselves. The results make it apparent whether we are modest drinkers, who need to be advised about safe drinking (AUDIT score of less than 7), or hazardous drinkers, who need to recognise their dangerous alcohol consumption (AUDIT score of between 8 and 15), or harmful drinkers, who are probably already damaging their physical or mental health (AUDIT score of between 16 and 19). An AUDIT score over 20 suggests that someone is drinking in a dependent or addicted way. Women and men in this category need to seek professional help, and to do this as soon as possible.

Of course, taking this AUDIT test is no substitute for a proper multidisciplinary assessment with qualified health professionals, but maybe you are not there yet. Maybe your whole new plan for living needs to go back to Step One – to contemplation before you act for a better way of living. AUDIT could help you to change the way you understand your consumption of alcohol. Maybe you have been contemplating cutting back, or considering cutting out your alcohol use? If so, the AUDIT tool might help you to decide what to do next.

So, as part of Step Ten of your whole new plan for living, what action do you need to take? If your AUDIT scores are on the hazardous end of the scale, you need to consider reducing your alcohol consumption – or maybe even abstaining – at least for some time. If your AUDIT score tells you that your alcohol use is already harmful, you need to consider stopping drinking, although you may need some form of counselling or continued monitoring if you are to do this successfully. Now might be the time to reach out to the fellowship of Alcoholics Anonymous or a similar group to find the support you will need. The collaboration you will find at AA could make a big difference. It could save your life.

Lastly, if you are in the dependent (addicted) region, you should seek specialist support immediately and look for further evaluation and treatment of your dependency.

Alcohol dependency is a disease and it can only be helped through intervention and measures to sustain abstinence. The more we discover about our use of alcohol, the better it will be for ourselves, our families and our society. A simple screening like the AUDIT test measure is one way of posing these important questions to ourselves about our relationship with alcohol. To progress with our whole new plan for living at this stage we need to answer honestly. What we do about our score after that is up to us. It's your plan for a whole new life.

Substance misuse (including misuse of a prescribed substance)

There is nothing new in our desire for something to ease our distress and calm us at times of difficulty. But is it ever legitimate for a doctor to prescribe a drug to meet this need?

This dilemma is a real one. Psychiatrists prescribe drugs with the intention of healing distress. The list of these drugs includes a variety of antidepressants, mood stabilisers, anxiolytics and antipsychotics, but is it appropriate to recommend these medicines to people experiencing common mental health difficulties? Maybe we ought to restrict these products to those with severe or enduring health problems. The answer, in my view, is that the use of prescription drugs is justified but it must continue to be evidence-based and audited.

Even substances that are potentially addictive can have a legitimate use, at least in the short term. Opiates such as morphine and codeine are good examples of these kinds of prescriptions. Benzodiazepines (BZDs such as Valium or Xanax) can have great value in treating drug withdrawal, epilepsy and in anaesthetic practice, but the long-term use of a BZD is not safe.

Benzodiazepines and the other so-called 'Z-drugs' (such as Zolpidem) should be used very briefly for insomnia but not in the medium or long term. These substances are highly addictive. Modern health services insist on adherence to strict prescribing guidelines, limiting their administration to appropriate cases, but people can become psychologically and physically dependent on these drugs very rapidly after starting to take them. Drug dependency costs lives. Misuse of prescription and over-the-counter painkilling drugs has become an enormous problem, especially in the USA where the dependency on and abuse of legal substances is a hazard as big as the abuse of alcohol, marijuana or cocaine. The promotion of synthetic opiates, such as Oxycontin, is surely one of the greatest pharma marketing scandals of the twenty-first century.[lxxiv]

So, is there a difference between legitimate therapeutic drug use and misuse of prescribed substances? In general, the distinction is obvious, but for others it may be a very fine line. It's not just about knowing which substance is legal, it's the intention of the prescription that matters – and this is crucial, along with continued monitoring and auditing of the evidence of a drug's benefit over its harm. Dependency on prescription drugs[lxxv] and over-the-counter painkillers cannot be part of our whole new plan for living.

Families of those on medications often ask me the hardest questions:

'Why is my loved one on all this medication?'; 'Who will take responsibility for the fact that my brother has become dependent on these prescribed drugs?'

Hard as these questions might be, we have reached a point where they must be answered, and so the proper use of pharmacotherapy must be justified and supported. Genuine science is the only source for such an answer.

Misuse of illicit substances and dependency on prescribed substances are two distinct problems. Neither is a matter of personal choice, but dependency on prescribed substances is insidious. It is marked by persistent side-effects and evidence of withdrawals. To address this we need to return to the scientific data and to be guided by real evidence of therapeutic benefit, whatever we are prescribed. As service users we must demand better information about the risks and the benefits of anything prescribed for us. This includes the risk of dependency.

Marijuana use

The so-called 'war on drugs' has failed. Our society's marijuana dependency is proof of this. Use of marijuana is now so widespread that attempts by governments to reduce its availability are a waste of time and money. Consequently, a growing number of nations have given up opposing personal use of marijuana. Many legislators have moved beyond decriminalising it and instead, have chosen to licence it. For example, recreational use of marijuana has been fully legalised in Canada.

And this is not just about Canada. Attitudes to the use of cannabis have changed almost everywhere. Each country has a different experience. Legalisation has been, for reasons more political than scientific, driven as much by libertarian frustrations as by public health concerns. So, should we still be concerned about marijuana use or about any other drug misuse for that matter? Why do people like me recommend that we use less marijuana? Why should cutting out the weed be part of your whole new plan for living?

To find an answer, it is best to go back to the scientific data. The active ingredient of marijuana is tetrahydrocannabinol, also known as THC. This lipid-like (fat-loving) substance dissolves in fatty tissue and so it interferes with normal brain development[lxxvi] in an enduring way.

The benign term 'weed' harkens back to the 1960s,

the era of Woodstock and a time when marijuana use was counter-cultural. Its use was politically charged, but the marijuana back then was relatively harmless. Today's marijuana is much higher in THC content and therefore much more potent, so the health concerns regarding the marijuana use of today are much greater. They relate to the increased volume of, and chronicity of exposure to, THC.

The harmful effects of marijuana use are the subject of much debate. They are both short term and long term and they include significant negative effects on the developing brain. Acute short-term negative effects include an altered sense of time, impaired movement, anxiety, hallucinations and delusions. The long-term harmful effects include impaired thinking, learning and memory. The latter effects are more likely when THC is taken for longer periods and in higher doses. Other important harmful effects include breathing difficulties, increased risk of strokes, and problems with pregnancy, such as low birth weight and developmental delay.

Some of us continue to highlight marijuana's harmful potential, but while others disagree, my reading of the data is that, compared to non-users, regular marijuana users have a lower satisfaction with life, poorer health and more difficulties in relationships. Despite this reading of the data, many people believe that marijuana is relatively harmless.[lxxvii] They argue that marijuana is no more dangerous than alcohol or other legally available psychoactive and addictive substances. To my mind, this is a fatuous argument. Relative harm is no longer the point. The reality is that regular use of high-potency marijuana is objectively harmful, but its prohibition has been neither effective nor beneficial for society. The answers to the health concerns about marijuana use lie in better education and improved systems of public health.

George Shultz and Pedro Aspe, writing in *The New York Times*,[lxxviii] put it well: 'We have a crisis on our hands – and for the past half-century, we have been failing to solve it. But there are alternatives ... We need to look beyond the idea that drug abuse is simply a law-enforcement problem, solvable through arrests, prosecution and restrictions on supply. We must attack it together with public health policies and education. We still have time to persuade our young people not to ruin their lives.'

If Shultz and Aspe are right, then Step Ten of our whole new plan means rethinking our use of substances, including marijuana.

Psychosis

The stress of everyday life is challenging, but for some people, life has an additional distress. This distress is called 'psychosis', a complete breakdown of someone's ability to recognise reality. Imagine how you would feel if your thoughts and your senses misled you all the time, and if for that reason you became unable to identify what was real or imagined. A failure of reality-testing is the characteristic feature of psychosis.

In good health, we rely on our senses – our sight, our hearing, our taste, our touch and our sense of smell – to identify our environment and our place within it. In psychosis, our senses misinform us, and this experience of misinformation changes the recognition of reality. The erroneous sensory experiences that arise in psychosis are called hallucinations. These can be strange, grandiose, frightening and even bizarre. The erroneous beliefs that arise in psychosis are called delusions and they are fixed and false and held unshakeably. They cannot be rationalised as arising from cultural or social norms.

Try to imagine how your thinking would change if your senses began to mislead you in this way, if you were to experience a life that was completely contrary to objective reality. Your interpretation of the world and your beliefs would inevitably change, if only to explain your particular experience. Sensations with no external validity (hallucinations), and false beliefs tenaciously held (delusions) are typical features of this psychosis.

At least 3 per cent of the population will experience a psychosis at some stage in their lifetime.[lxxix] For some people, psychosis is a time-limited experience that is prompted by an acute brain illness or by substance misuse. For others, it is part of an enduring or relapsing mental health disorder, such as temporal lobe epilepsy, acquired brain injury, bipolar mood disorder or schizophrenia.

Of course, it would not be correct to say that all unusual sensory experiences are indicative of psychosis. Many people 'hear voices' without an external source, and they do so without any enduring mental health disorder. In Ireland the Hearing Voices Network,[lxxx] which is part of an international movement, is dedicated to the recognition of this remarkable fact.

Similarly, many people have unusual beliefs and they hold them with intensity and without much objective evidence, but these beliefs are not in themselves an indication of any mental disorder or psychosis.

Like every other mental health diagnosis, the term 'psychosis' refers to a set of symptoms, and these need to be seen within the context of a whole life. Symptoms are only a problem if they reach a certain threshold, one in which they interfere with the ability to function, to live, to love and to work. Psychotic symptoms may be persistent, pervasive and profoundly disturbing of human function. We need to know much more about why psychosis occurs and how to help people who experience it; we also need to understand why this condition is still so feared and so neglected.

Psychotic experience is overrepresented among the poor, the young, the homeless and the imprisoned; all of these groups experience increased societal prejudice. Hostility to those living with psychosis is one of the least acknowledged and persistent prejudices worldwide.

In addition to this marginalisation and alienation there is another real problem for those with psychosis: it is fear. Psychosis, by its nature, is hard to comprehend and so it is as frightening for families and friends as it is for those who experience it personally. It would be better if we addressed this fear with better education and more skills. If our community is expected to care for those with enduring mental health problems, then the community needs to be helped to understand.

Perhaps the biggest problem for those with psychosis and other enduring mental health difficulties is our collective pessimism. There is a widespread belief that people with psychosis cannot really be helped. This is a colossal error. The reality is that recovery from psychosis is possible, and today's evidence-based mental health services provide the most effective ways of achieving this. We know that early intervention for psychosis is effective,[lxxxi] but interventionist mental health services in Ireland and around the world remain patchy, fragmented and often far too difficult to access. Isolated areas of best practice do exist, but there are huge gaps and delay is typical. This delay has a detrimental effect on recovery.

Shine (formerly Schizophrenia Ireland) advocates for services and the rights of people with enduring mental health problems in Ireland, including psychosis. An equivalent organisation in the UK, Rethink Mental Illness,[lxxxii] sums the situation up well: 'If your motor car has a breakdown today, it is likely that it will be fixed today, but if you or one of your family has a mental breakdown today, it is likely to be eighteen months before they receive any care.'

We need the capacity to deliver the full range of modern, effective treatments fit for the twenty-first century without delay. In Step Ten of our whole new plan we must reduce delays, we will not postpone care, and we won't hesitate to reach out to each other for the care we need.

Post-traumatic stress disorder

On 15 January 2009, Captain Chesley 'Sully' Sullenberger and First Officer Jeff Skiles landed US Airways Flight 1549 onto the Hudson River, near Manhattan in New York. All one hundred and fifty-five passengers and crew were rescued safely. The event is almost unprecedented in aviation history: dual-engine failure arising from a collision with a flock of geese, followed by successful landing of an Airbus A320 on urban water with no loss of life.

Captain Sullenberger was instantly hailed a 'hero' in public, a status he earned firstly because of the scale of his achievement and subsequently by the intelligence and humility of his performance in the media. An interview on the CBS TV show *60 Minutes* reinforced the public perception that he is an exceptional man. Although Sullenberger did not seek his 'hero' status, he recognised the public's real need for hope. 'They want good news,' he said.

The subsequent movie, *Sully*, starring Tom Hanks and directed by Clint Eastwood, is hard to categorise. It is part disaster movie and part courtroom drama, but I like to see it as a film about mental health, as it examines in detail the phenomenon of post-traumatic stress disorder (PTSD). A stress-induced mental health disorder, PTSD can affect anyone following an extreme stress, but typically occurs after a life-threatening event. The person exposed to an extreme trauma develops a series of characteristic phenomena, including hypervigilance, avoidance behaviour and a re-experiencing of the trauma. These re-experiences are referred to as 'flashbacks'. In *Sully*, we have a cinematic and psychological visualisation of the effects of extreme stress on an ordinary man doing an ordinary job on an extraordinary day. The drama is about his symptoms of insomnia, guilt and anxiety and his terrifying recollections of this shocking, traumatic event. Like so many acute traumas, the sheer rapidity of the events posed another problem for Sullenberger himself. He explains to his co-pilot Skiles that 'forty years of my flying experience will be judged on just 200 seconds of flight time'. In his PTSD he discovers that his experience of these traumatic events is recurrent. Many survivors describe this. The problem with PTSD, they tell me, is that 'the trauma isn't over – it just keeps happing again and again'.

These re-experiences are painful recollections and they enter the mind despite every attempt to dismiss them. Such distressing flashbacks are characteristic of an acute stress reaction and they are vivid and terrifying in themselves. They are akin to the relived experiences illustrated in the film, where in roughly ninety minutes we see more than twenty versions of the Airbus crash. For Captain Sullenberger, the events are prompted to re-occur repeatedly, in his dreams or while awake, by random reminders during his agonising periods of self-doubt and self-examination.

Vivid flashbacks are not the only post-traumatic stress phenomenon depicted in this film. For a time, Sullenberger is shown as isolated and avoidant, insomniac and hypervigilant, and often full of guilt. His experiences persist for some time, despite the support of his passengers and crew, his wife and his family. The cockpit of his plane becomes a visual metaphor for his mind and for the private mental experience of this near-catastrophic reality.

His vindication before the airline authorities becomes less significant than his own personal recovery achieved through radical acceptance of this experience. This dramatic narrative of relived events mimics modern trauma-focused cognitive behavioural therapy. The film, without ever making an explicit reference to it, shows that re-exposure to feared events[lxxxiii] can lead to recovery.

Just before the verdict is announced, and having witnessed many repeated simulations of the events, Sullenberger asks for a brief recess to speak with his co-pilot, Skiles, to say that he has come to his own view that they had both acted properly – and this is what matters. Before they return to the courtroom, Sullenberger thanks his co-pilot and commends him for being with him through it all. In this the film hints at something we have come to know about successful modern therapy for PTSD: that radical acceptance, commitment and self-compassion are keys to this recovery.

Sadly, PTSD is not a rare or exceptional problem; indeed traumatic stress disorders are very common. Many people develop these stress disorders and they often struggle for long periods trying to find some personal understanding of the events that happened to them. Too few people have access to meaningful therapy after traumatic events and so many remain stuck in a personal suffering that keeps recurring. This may or may not be relevant to your whole new plan, but I think it could be. In any case, we must try to be more open about the reality of traumatic stress disorders and more vocal about the prospect of their successful treatment.

Stress-related difficulties of workers

People sometimes ask whether doctors are different from other people when it comes to stress, distress and mental health disorder. Do doctors and nurses suffer more or less? Do they have different problems? Are they more or less likely to get help and recover? The truthful answer, as with so many health-related questions, is not straightforward.

Doctors and other healthcare workers are likely to have as many physical and mental health issues as anyone else, but there is some evidence that, when it comes to stress-related problems and addictions, their problems are even greater than those of others in the community. Doctors are regularly exposed to additional traumas as part of their work, so their experiences are not like everyone else's. This additional risk of exposure to trauma is something they share with other first responders, such as fire officers and the police, and with other clinical workers, most notably nurses and allied health professionals.

Unsurprisingly, doctors in the emergency room are more at risk of stress-related disorders than those in less acute settings. Their trauma is often prolonged and hidden from public view: mental suffering and addictions in the clinical professions are concealed experiences. Disclosure is especially hazardous for doctors, as it adds the risk of professional jeopardy to the problems of shame and guilt. The recent COVID-19 pandemic has made this more obvious. Burnout of clinical staff is a major problem and reducing this is a collective responsibility. Well-managed practices and clinical services have an interest in maintaining the health of their staff.

The culture of the health organisation may also be a factor. Some services are better than others at maintaining the mental welfare of their clinical staff. In 2013 in the UK Sir Robert Francis reported on the deaths of hundreds of patients in the care of the Mid Staffordshire Hospital. The deaths arose from poor care. His report emphasised the importance of kindness within the health service, for both staff and patients. He found that a hospital with a culture that is unkind to its staff is more likely to have staff that are unkind to their patients and to each other. Caring is a reciprocal and a cultural thing. An unkind health culture cannot be an effective culture of caring[lxxxiv] and so in Mid Staffordshire many lives were lost as a result.

Healthcare workers are human beings with real personal problems and genuine stresses, but awareness of this is not as widespread as it should be.[lxxxv] The public still places the medical profession at the top of the ladder of trustworthiness – even more so since the start of the COVID-19 pandemic – but the public image and the harsh reality of a clinician's professional life are not necessarily well matched. Maintenance of this iconic respect for doctors in the community comes at the cost of real disclosure about the health of our clinical staff.

The changing image of doctors in the media suggests a real shift in perceptions is underway. In my youth, in the 1960s, doctors were portrayed in the cinema and on television as reliable, avuncular figures who instantly commanded great respect; they were also invariably male. By contrast, modern television doctors depicted in TV shows like *Scrubs* or *House* or *Grey's Anatomy* are less reliable and often much more troubled people. The picture of today's television doctors reveals more alarming psychological needs than before. Perhaps there is progress in this.

This change in the portrayal of the medical profession comes at the same time as a change of attitude among the medical regulatory authorities. Demands for greater governance, prompted in the UK by the Harold Shipman scandal,[lxxxvi] have shifted the emphasis away from the support of the doctor towards the protection of the public from the doctor. This is a good thing, but it risks leaving the sick doctor and particularly those with mental health issues in a potentially lonely space.

The biblical dictum 'Physician, heal thyself'[lxxxvii] comes to mind. Many doctors continue to practise without a GP/doctor for their own health needs. Each one of us (including every doctor) needs a personal health plan. Many of us could do with making a whole new plan for living. Recovery for the healthcare worker starts with the same steps that work for everyone else, but in the case of the clinician there is always someone else to consider and that is the patient. It stands to reason that a doctor or a nurse who is well themselves will be much better at their job. A whole new plan for living could make a great difference to the doctor or nurse and to their patients.

A greater practical understanding of the work–life balance would also be helpful, as in Step Four of our whole new plan for living. This is not yet widespread among the medical profession. Doctors, like some hospital management, have been slow to accept that they need quality sleep just like everyone else. Demands for a work–time initiative limiting the numbers of hours worked by an average physician were resisted by some in the profession. One colleague of mine used to groan to me about his work–life balance by saying: 'Why must I have all the work, while my colleagues have all the balance?'

Thankfully, leaders in the profession are doing more now to promote health awareness, starting at medical school, and this is building at professional levels through colleges and societies. In Ireland, there is an independent professional health facility called Practitioner Health[lxxxviii] and the regulator, the Medical Council,[lxxxix] has incorporated a Health Committee with responsibility for doctors' wellbeing. This group works within a framework of respect for patient safety.

There is still much work to be done in this regard, but progress is being made. Mental distress and disorder are at least as common, at least as preventable and at least as treatable in the clinical professions as they are in the community. Modern mental healthcare should be more accessible for those who do the caring. Neglect is not an option.

So does this matter? What, if anything, has this got to do with your whole new plan for living? It could mean a great deal if you are one of the many thousands who work in the healthcare professions. And even if you're not one of those, it's worth remembering that a significant part of everybody's recovery depends on the maintenance of healthy caring professionals. Healthcare employees care for the sick and often this includes those working in the caring professions. Modern healthcare systems depend on human teams, and so there is a need for doctors, nurses, psychologists and other healthcare professions to work together. Their needs must be acknowledged and addressed. We have moved away from an old male medical fantasy towards a new diverse and human reality. The twenty-first-century healthcare professional will be a better healer if we care for them and help them to take care of themselves.

Deliberate self-harm

One in five young people in Ireland has self-harmed by the time they reach the age of eighteen.[xc] These attempts at self-injury are not easily classified or understood, but one thing is certain – self-harming behaviour is not a mental illness. It is a destructive behaviour and its causes are as diverse as the individuals who self-harm.

Deliberate self-injury has become one of the most common reasons people attend hospital emergency departments in Ireland or the UK.[xci] Although there is still much to understand about self-harm, some facts are emerging that have begun to inform us of the importance of this problem.

The motivations for deliberate self-harm are varied, ranging from an urgent need to regulate emotional distress to a rehearsal of a suicidal intent. Just as there is no single cause for self-harm, there is also no single explanation for it either. Self-harm is not a benign behaviour and it is a mistake to dismiss it simply as a gesture or a 'cry for help'. Half of those who ultimately die by suicide have previously self-harmed, and the life expectancy of men who self-harm is reduced by nearly 50 per cent.[xcii]

The main form of self-harm seen in hospital admissions is self-poisoning (often described incorrectly as an 'overdose'). In the community, many more forms of self-harming behaviours continue unnoticed, the most common being self-cutting. Many of these self-injuries are inflicted at home, work or school, and in young people most recur without any adult being aware of them. Self-harm is a repeated behaviour. At least one fifth of those who repeatedly self-harm will do so again within the next twelve months.

The most effective way to reduce self-harm is to reduce its repetition. Unfortunately, so far, the efforts of mental healthcare systems in this regard have not been coherent.[xciii] Our therapeutic approach to self-harm needs to be redesigned. We could start by focusing our initiatives on two areas: in the community (especially in schools) and in the hospitals.

Awareness-raising initiatives in schools are very effective methods of reducing self-harming behaviour. Many people fear that schools will be places of contagion, and they worry about copycat behaviours or a cluster of self-harming school children. However, it is more likely that schools are becoming places of recovery and enlightenment. Young people respond well to school initiatives that highlight positive mental health awareness. These efforts in schools can have a dramatic effect on reducing self-harming behaviours.

Teachers are some of the most important channels of mental and behavioural health awareness, and they need greater support. The skills needed to enhance their ability can be amplified relatively quickly. There is evidence that even after just two days of training, teachers are better equipped to prepare themselves for these challenges.

Those who come to attention in hospital following an episode of self-harm or self-poisoning and who receive even a single professional mental health assessment do better than those who do not. The same is also true for those referred for evidence-based problem-solving therapies, like mindfulness-based cognitive behavioural therapy or interpersonal therapy.

Unfortunately, too few people attending the emergency departments are offered an assessment. There is still no standard offering of psychotherapy to people with self-harming behaviour, as is recommended by the best clinical guidelines.[xciv]

So, what should we do about deliberate self-harm? How should we respond as parents, family, teachers and friends of those who jeopardise themselves in this way? Could this be a part of our whole new plan for living? My answer to this is yes, but the next question is how?

The first response is to listen. It is very distressing to discover that someone you love is harming themselves. This behaviour is dangerous, but if we can reframe the discovery (Step Nine) and think of the new awareness of it as being something good (Steps Three to Six), we can start to help. This may be the first opportunity we have had to hear about the issues and to offer some effective support. This is not a place for blame or shame, not a time for pull-yourself-together platitudes. Everyone presenting to the emergency department with deliberate self-harm deserves an opportunity to talk about their problem with a counsellor or trained therapist. People who harm themselves should seek professional assistance, or at the very least some form of assessment. Some people with self-harming issues will resolve their problems simply by being offered this help; others benefit from more prolonged therapy and treatment. But in our whole new plan for living, neglect is not an option. In Step Ten of our whole new plan we will try to promote a greater awareness of mental health and to acknowledge its value to our new wellbeing. We can do this throughout our lives and in many settings. Programmes to reduce stigma within schools have been shown to be effective, as have community initiatives[xcv] focusing on resilience and mindfulness. Stigma and fear can be overcome. Much good work is being carried out in Ireland by organisations like Pieta House,[xcvi] but so much more still needs to be done. Self-harm may be a symptom of greater problems people are having in our homes, schools and communities. We have an opportunity to address these difficulties by making our whole new plan for living.

Epilogue

So, what about my own whole new plan for living?
Like you, I have been looking for new ways to live well.
Hopefully in this book we have been exploring these
ways together, collaborating in the mutual discovery
of our unique plan. For me that means learning how
to be well and how to stay well while going through
lots of change in my life and in my work, including
retiring from a busy managerial role and moving to
a different, more clinical one. I have been very lucky.
It's been a challenging time for so many people, trying
to maintain their balance through the pandemic while

coping with the complex dynamics of life. So, in my turn I have been re-evaluating things and making my own whole new plan by setting it out in this book. Like the Irish airman in the quote at the start of this book, I have been balancing things and bringing them all to mind. Among many other things, I have taken the opportunity to join a band of musicians, made up of a group of my friends who are also in search of renewed wellness. It's been fun to be with them.

We call ourselves – somewhat tentatively – 'The Art of Collaboration'. We meet to make music, to laugh, to read and to think about new ways of doing things. During the lockdowns, we Zoomed and called and collaborated with each other online. Like so many other people, we tried to live more hopefully (and social media helped us to connect). We have no leader, although there are many leaders among us. We have no prescription, although there are some of us who could prescribe. We have only one commitment: to collaborate with each other, and by working and playing together, to experience the transience of what we do. Maybe you think this is just play-acting, just an answer to my midlife crisis, but I like to see it as an acknowledgement of something: that we are all in this together, all in search of wellness and all learning to go with the flow.

Collaboration is not our end, but it is a vital part of our plan for a whole new way of living. Sharing this time has been rewarding. We enjoy ourselves. Our experience continues despite the complexity, the volatility and the uncertainty of the life that surrounds us. Coming together and performing helps us in our distress. It is a part of our fellowship. In this way our recovery can be individual and collective, and as we play together and increase our resilience as individuals, we build a recovery for ourselves and sustain it for one another.

Central to this plan for a more hopeful future is a willingness to collaborate with other people. People can collaborate anywhere – in sports at any level, through hobbies or gardening, in choirs, by homemaking or at the gym. Wherever there is a community, there is potential for a collaboration, and this takes us beyond our nuclear confines to that extra support that sustained us even through the lockdown.

With a whole new plan for living, we can learn to love and to be loved together, and so we can go on loving one another for as long as we are able. We can come together in many more sustainable ways. This collaboration will be fruitful – though it won't always be easy – and through it we will address the misunderstood parts of our lives. Overcoming our difficulties in this way will be a route to what I like to call the therapy of the self; through a collaboration with others we learn to integrate ourselves. Our awareness of today contains within it the awareness of our past and a barely hidden anxiety about our future, but whatever is to happen to us, in our future and to our world, we will be better for experiencing it together.

This has been our time for making a whole new plan for living. Thank you for allowing me to share it with you. Now is your time for living. For the past thirty-five years it has been my professional privilege to witness all kinds of recovery and to see people living this recovery again and again and day after day. Through collaboration people can move from distress to calmness, from despair to hope, and from awareness to action for better health. This is my witness and it has been my experience. Now I hope that it becomes the shared goal of your whole new plan for living.

Acknowledgements

Writing is a personal and a collaborative enterprise and so I am very grateful to all those who encouraged me to start writing this book and those who helped me to complete it. Special thanks must go to Sheila Crowley of Curtis Brown, who believed in it from its beginning, and Ciara Doorley at Hachette Ireland, who helped me see it through to its finish.

Many others helped me, and it would be impossible to mention them all by name; some read drafts of the text and some advised me on specific content, but all gave freely from their stores of wisdom. I am grateful to

Charlotte Frorath for her insights, and to my patients and my colleagues and friends at St Patrick's University Hospital. Among these I want to mention Tom Maher, Paul Gilligan, John Creedon, James Braddock, Colman Noctor, Anne Donnelly, Catherine Hughes, Jenny Corr, Natasha Oliveira, Tamara Nolan, Sarah Surgenor, Niamh O'Reilly and many others among the nurses, doctors and allied professionals who make up our multidisciplinary teams and with whom I have worked for so many happy years.

I wrote this book during the first COVID-19 lockdown, when the whole world seemed to be turning upside-down. Friends and family played a huge part in helping me to focus on it, to maintain my momentum and to continue to see the value of the project. I wish to pay specific tribute to Patrick Stephenson, John Hillery, Conor Killeen, Seamus Brett, Paul Roe, Liam Hennessy, Edward Neale, Niamh Clarke, Peter McGivern, Vincent Ryan, Karen Leonard, Padraig Wright and Sarah Delaney.

Lastly and most importantly I want to thank my wife and children, my brother and my sisters for their love and support during this and many other projects.

Bibliography

Balint, M., *The Doctor, His Patient and the Illness*, 2nd edn (Pitman Paperbacks, 1968)

Beck, A.T., *Cognitive Therapy and the Emotional Disorders* (Plume, 1979)

Dalai Lama, The, and Stril-Rever, S., *My Spiritual Journey* (Harper One, 2011)

Damasio, A., *Descartes' Error: Emotion, Reason and the Human Brain* (Vintage, 2006)

Daniel, B. and Wassell, S., *Assessing and Promoting Resilience in Vulnerable Children* (Jessica Kingsley Publishers, 2002)

Frankl, V.E., *Man's Search for Meaning* (Washington Square Press, 1959)

Freud, S., *The Interpretation of Dreams: The Complete and Definitive Text*, trans. by J. Strachey (Basic Books, 1955)

Gilbert, P., *Compassion Focused Therapy (CBT Distinctive Features)* (Routledge, 2010)

Goldman, B., *The Power of Kindness: Why Empathy Is Essential in Everyday Life* (HarperCollins Publishers, 2018)

Harrison, A.F. and Bramson, R.M., *The Art of Thinking: The Classic Guide to Increasing Brain Power* (Berkley Books, 2002)

Headon, A., *The Power of YES: Positive and Practical Advice To Help You Live Life to the Full* (Ilex Press, 2018)

Kabat-Zinn, J., *Full Catastrophe Living: How To Cope with Stress, Pain and Illness Using Mindfulness Meditation*, revised edn (Piatkus, 2013)

Kandel, E., *Psychiatry, Psychoanalysis, and the New Biology of Mind* (American Psychiatric Publishing, 2005)

Kelly, B., *The Doctor Who Sat for a Year* (Gill Books, 2019)

Kohen, D., *Oxford Textbook of Women and Mental Health* (Oxford University Press, 2010)

Lewis, C.S., *A Grief Observed*, new edn (Faber & Faber, 2013)

Lynch, T., *The Undertaking: Life Studies from the Dismal Trade* (Vintage, 1998)

Marks, I., *Fears, Phobias and Rituals: Panic, Anxiety, and Their Disorders* (Oxford University Press, 1987)

Maslach, M., *Burnout: The Cost of Caring* (Malor Books, 2003)

Miller, D.P., *The Forgiveness Book: Healing the Hurts We Don't Deserve* (Hampton Roads Publishing, 2017)

Mitchell, D., *Thinking About It Only Makes It Worse: And Other Lessons from Modern Life* (Faber Publishing, 2015)

Peale, N.V., *The Power of Positive Thinking*, reprint edn (Touchstone, 2003)

Stevenson, R.L., *Essays of Travel* (Chatto & Windus, 1905)

Taylor, D.M. et al., *The Maudsley Prescribing Guidelines in Psychiatry*, 13th edn (Wiley-Blackwell, 2018)

Vaillant, G.E., *Triumphs of Experience: The Men of the Harvard Grant Study*, reprint edn (Belknap Press, 2015)

Wellings, K. et al., *Sexual Health: A Public Health Perspective (Understanding Public Health)* (Open University Press, 2012)

Winnicott, D.W., 'The Theory of the Parent–Infant Relationship', *International Journal of Psychoanalysis*, vol. 41, 1960, pp. 585–95

Endnotes

i   Organisation for Economic Co-operation and Development, *Health at a Glance: Europe 2018* (OECD, 2018).

ii   M. Swarbrick, 'A Wellness Approach', *Psychiatric Rehabilitation Journal*, vol. 29, pp. 311–14.

iii   J. Aked et al., *Five Ways to Wellbeing*, a report presented to the Foresight Project on communicating the evidence base for improving people's wellbeing (Centre for Wellbeing, the New Economics Foundation, 2008).

iv   M. Leamy et al., 'Conceptual Framework for Personal Recovery in Mental Health: Systematic Review and Narrative Synthesis (CHIME)', *The British Journal of Psychiatry*, vol. 199, 2011, pp. 445–52.

v   M. Hughes et al., 'Prevalence of Psychological Distress in General Practitioner Adult Attendees', *Clinical Psychology Forum*, vol. 206, 2010, pp. 33–8.

vi   T. Vos et al., 'Global, Regional and National Incidence, Prevalence and Years Lived with Disability for 301 Acute and Chronic Diseases and Injuries in 188 Countries, 1990–2013: A Systematic Analysis for the Global Burden of Disease Study 2013', *The Lancet*, vol. 386, no. 9995, 2015, pp. 743–800.

vii   M. Marmot, 'Social Determinants of Health Inequalities', *The Lancet*, vol. 365, no. 9464, 2005, pp. 1099–1104.

viii   M. Linehan, *DBT Skills Training Manual*, 2nd edn (Guilford Press, 2014).

ix   P. Barker and P. Buchanan-Barker, *Spirituality and Mental Health: Breakthrough* (Wiley, 2006).

x   J. Chozen Bays, *Mindful Eating: A Guide to Rediscovering a Healthy and Joyful Relationship with Food* (Shambhala, 2009).

xi   M. Walker, *Why We Sleep: The New Science of Sleep and Dreams* (Penguin, 2018).

xii   M.T. de Mello et al., 'Sleep Disorders as a Cause of Motor Vehicle Collisions', *International Journal of Preventive Medicine*, vol. 4, no. 3, 2013, pp. 246–57.

xiii   C. Hibbert, *8 Keys to Mental Health Through Exercise* (W.W. Norton & Co., 2016).

xiv   T. Fahey, R. Layte and B. Gannon, *Sports Participation and Health among Adults in Ireland*, The Economic and Social Research Institute, Dublin, 2004.

xv   E. Bullmore, *The Inflamed Mind: A Radical New Approach to Depression* (Short Books, 2019).

xvi   B. Kelly, *The Doctor Who Sat for a Year* (Gill Books, 2019).

xvii   The ICD-10 Classification of Mental and Behavioural Disorders (WHO): Code F33: Major depressive disorder, recurrent.

xviii   S. Bachmann, 'Epidemiology of Suicide and the Psychiatric Perspective', *International Journal of Environmental Research and Public Health*, vol. 15, no. 1425, 2018, p. 92.

xix   A.H. Maslow, 'Hierarchy of Needs: A Theory of Human Motivation', *Psychological Review*, vol. 50, no. 4, 1943.

xx   M. Marmot, *Social Determinants of Health*, 2nd edn (Oxford University Press, 2005).

xxi   C. Noctor, *Cop On: What It Is and Why Your Child Needs It To Survive and Thrive in Today's World* (Gill Books, 2015).

xxii   A.T. Beck, *Cognitive Therapy and the Emotional Disorders* (Plume, 1979).

xxiii   J. Kim-Cohen et al., 'Prior Juvenile Diagnoses in Adults with Mental Disorder: Developmental Follow-Back of a Prospective-Longitudinal Cohort', *Archives of General Psychiatry*, vol. 60, no. 7, 2003, pp. 709–17; B. Dooley and A. Fitzgerald, *My World Study: National Study of Youth Mental Health in Ireland* (Headstrong/UCD School of Psychology, 2012), https://researchrepository.ucd.ie/handle/10197/4286.

xxiv   Workplace Relations Commission, *Guide to Employment, Labour and Equality Law*.

xxv   A. O'Duffy, *A Guide to the Law in Ireland in Relation to Disability* (Independent Living Movement Ireland, 2018).

xxvi   C. Maslach and S. Jackson, 'The Measurement of Experienced Burnout', *Journal of Organizational Behaviour*, vol. 2, no. 2, 1981, pp. 99–113.

xxvii   D.A. Sbarra, 'Divorce and Health: Current Trends and Future Directions', *Psychosomatic Medicine*, vol. 77, 2015, pp. 227–36.

xxviii   Ibid.

xxix   G. Vaillant, *Triumphs of Experience* (Harvard University Press, 2015).

xxx   E. Kübler-Ross, *On Death and Dying*, reprint edn (Scribner, 2011).

xxxi   T. Lynch, *The Undertaking: Life Studies from the Dismal Trade* (Vintage, 1998).

xxxii   National Office for Suicide Prevention (NOSP), *Briefing on CSO Suicide Figures, 4th November 2020* (NOSP, 2020).

xxxiii   B. McManus, *Redemption Road: Grieving on the Camino* (Orpen Press, 2017).

xxxiv   C.-K. Chang et al., 'Life Expectancy at Birth for People with Serious Mental Illness and other Major Disorders', *PLOS ONE*, vol. 6, no. 5, 2011.

xxxv   M. Balint, *The Doctor, His Patient and the Illness*, 2nd edn (Pitman Paperbacks, 1968).

xxxvi   S. Freud, *An Outline of Psycho-Analysis* (W.W. Norton & Co., 1989).

xxxvii   J. Lucey, *The Life Well Lived: Therapeutic Paths to Recovery and Wellbeing* (Transworld, 2018).

xxxviii   D. Greenberger, *Mind Over Mood: Change How You Feel by Changing the Way You Think*, 2nd edn (Guilford Press, 2015).

xxxix   E.H. Erikson and J.M. Erikson, *The Life Cycle Completed* (W.W. Norton & Co., 1998).

xl   D. Kohen, *Oxford Textbook of Women and Mental Health* (Oxford University Press, 2010).

xli   Ibid.

xlii   P. Gilligan, 'Deep Stigma Surrounding Mental Health Costs Lives' (2012), https://www.independent.ie/opinion/analysis/paul-gilligan-deep-stigma-surrounding-mental-health-costs-lives-28813002.html.

xliii   Organisation for Economic Co-operation and Development, *Health at a Glance, 2020* (OECD, 2020).

xliv   Organisation for Economic Co-operation and Development, *Health at a Glance: Europe 2018.*

xlv   T.R. Reid, 'Norwegian Prime Minister Wins Support By Publicizing His Depression', *Washington Post*, 25 October 1998.

xlvi   Mental Health in America, *The State of Mental Health in America*, https://www.mhanational.org/issues/state-mental-health-america; Substance Abuse and Mental Health Services Administration (SAMHSA), *National Survey on Drug Use and Health*, www.samhsa.gov.

xlvii   Organisation for Economic Co-operation and Development, *Health at a Glance, 2019* (OECD, 2019).

xlviii   Central Statistics Office, *System of Health Accounts, 2018* (CSO, Ireland, 2020).

xlix   M.E. Porter, *Redefining Health Care: Creating Value-Based Competition on Results* (Harvard Business School Press, 2006).

l   P. McVerry, *The Meaning Is in the Shadows* (Veritas Books, 2003).

li   D. Edmondson and R. von Känel, 'Post-traumatic Stress Disorder and Cardiovascular Disease', *Lancet Psychiatry*, vol. 4, no. 4, 2017, pp. 320–9.

lii   H. Selye, 'Stress and Disease', *Science*, vol. 122, no. 3171, 1955, pp. 625–31.

liii   J. Kabat-Zinn, *Full Catastrophe Living: How To Cope with Stress, Pain and Illness Using Mindfulness Meditation*, revised edn (Piatkus, 2013).

liv   V.E. Frankl, *Man's Search for Meaning* (Washington Square Press, 1959).

lv   C. Rogers, *Carl Rogers on Personal Power: Inner Strength and Its Revolutionary Impact* (Trans-Atlantic Publications, 1978).

lvi   M. Ward, R. Layte and R.A. Kenny, *Loneliness, Social Isolation, and Their Discordance among Older Adults: Findings from the Irish Longitudinal Study on Ageing* (TILDA) (Tilda, 2019).

lvii   Greenberger, *Mind Over Mood*. See Foreword by Aaron T. Beck.

lviii   J. Martin, *Jesus: A Pilgrimage* (Bravo Ltd, 2016).

lix   M. Foucault, *The Care of the Self*, trans by R. Hurley (Penguin, 1990).

lx   Frankl, *Man's Search for Meaning*.

lxi   J.C. Franklyn et al., 'Risk Factors for Suicidal Thoughts and Behaviors: A Meta-Analysis of 50 Years of Research', *Psychological Bulletin*, vol. 143, no. 2, 2017, pp. 187–232.

lxii   J.M. Schwartz and R. Gladding, *You Are Not Your Brain: The 4-Step Solution for Changing Bad Habits, Ending Unhealthy Thinking, and Taking Control of Your Life* (Avery Publishing Group, 2012).

lxiii   G. Roberts and P. Wolfson, 'The Rediscovery of Recovery: Open to All', *Advances in Psychiatric Treatment*, vol. 10, 2004, pp. 37–49.

lxiv   B. Daniel and S. Wassell, *Assessing and Promoting Resilience in Vulnerable Children* (Jessica Kingsley Publishers, 2002).

lxv   World Health Organisation, *Depression* (WHO, 2020).

lxvi   J. O'Doherty et al., 'The Prevalence and Treatment of Mental Health Conditions Documented in General Practice in Ireland', *Irish Journal of Psychological Medicine*, vol. 37, no. 1, 2020, pp. 24–31.

lxvii   S.L. Burcusa and W.G. Iacono, 'Risk for Recurrence in Depression', *Clinical Psychological Review*, vol. 27, no. 8, 2007, pp. 959–85.

lxviii   'Massive Increase in Prescribing Antidepressants in Ireland', *RTÉ Investigates* (RTÉ, 2019).

lxix   C. Rogers and R. Farson, *Active Listening* (Martino Publishing, 2015).

lxx   Alcohol Action Ireland, *Alcohol Facts, 2020*, https:// alcoholireland.ie/facts.

lxxi   V. Bagnardi et al., 'Alcohol Consumption and the Risk of Cancer: A Meta-Analysis', *Alcohol Res Health*, vol. 25, no. 4, 2001, pp. 263–70.

lxxii   R. Burton and N. Sheron, 'No Level of Alcohol Consumption Improves Health', *The Lancet*, vol. 392, no. 10152, 2018, pp. 987–8.

lxxiii   https://auditscreen.org.

lxxiv   *British Medical Journal*, 'Purdue Pharma To Plead Guilty and Pay $8.3bn over Opioid Marketing' (2020), https://www.bmj.com/content/371/bmj.m4103.

lxxv   *British Medical Journal*, 'Tackle Prescription Drug Dependency with Improved Clinician Training, Says Review' (2019), https://www.bmj.com/content/366/bmj.l5497/rr-0.

lxxvi   A. Berenon, *Tell Your Children: The Truth About Marijuana, Mental Illness and Violence* (Free Press, 2019).

lxxvii   D.W. Lachenmeier, 'Comparative Risk Assessment of Alcohol, Tobacco, Cannabis and Other Illicit Drugs Using the Margin of Exposure Approach', *Scientific Reports*, vol. 5, no. 1, 2015.

lxxviii G.P. Shultz and P. Aspe, 'The Failed War on Drugs', *New York Times*, 31 December 2017, https://www.nytimes.com/2017/12/31/opinion/failed-war-on-drugs.html.

lxxix   Z. Steel et al., 'The Global Prevalence of Common Mental Disorders: A Systematic Review and Meta-analysis, 1980–2013', *International Journal of Epidemiology*, vol. 43, no. 2, 2014, pp. 476–93.

lxxx   http://hearingvoicesnetworkireland.ie/

lxxxi   P.D. McGorry, E. Killackey and A.R. Yung, 'Early Intervention in Psychotic Disorders: Detection and Treatment of the First Episode and the Critical Early Stages', *Medical Journal of Australia*, vol. 187, no. 7, 2007, s. 8, https://www.mja.com.au/journal/2007/187/7/early-intervention-psychotic-disorders-detection-and-treatment-first-episode-and.

lxxxii   Rethink Mental Illness (National Schizophrenia Fellowship UK), rethink.org.

lxxxiii C.C. Engel, 'Review: Multiple-Session Trauma-Focused CBT within 3 Months of Event Reduces Symptoms in Acute Stress Disorder and PTSD', https://ebm.bmj.com/content/14/4/107.

lxxxiv J. Ballatt and P. Campling, *Intelligent Kindness: Reforming the Culture of Healthcare* (RCPsych Publications, 2011).

lxxxv B. Hayes et al., 'What's Up, Doc? A National Cross-Sectional Study of Psychological Wellbeing of Hospital Doctors in Ireland', https://bmjopen.bmj.com/content/7/10/e018023.

lxxxvi T. Jackson and R. Smith, 'Harold Shipman: A General Practitioner and Murderer', https://www.bmj.com/content/328/7433/231.

lxxxvii *The Bible* (New International Version), Luke 4:23, 'Physician, Heal Thyself'.

lxxxviii 'Looking After Your Wellbeing in Confidence', practitionerhealth.ie.

lxxxix 'Your Health Matters', Health Sub-Committee, Irish Medical Council, medicalcouncil.ie.

xc Dooley and Fitzgerald, *My World Study*; M. Cannon et al., *The Mental Health of Young People in Ireland: A Report of the Psychiatric Epidemiology Research across the Lifespan (PERL) Group* (Royal College of Surgeons in Ireland, 2013).

xci K. Bilén et al., 'Deliberate Self-harm Patients in the Emergency Department: Factors Associated with Repeated Self-harm among 1,524 Patients', *Emergency Medicine Journal*, vol. 28, 2011, pp. 1019–25.

xcii National Institute for Health and Clinical Excellence, 'Self-Harm: The Short-term Physical Management and Secondary Prevention of Self-Harm in Primary and Secondary Care' (2004), https://pubmed.ncbi.nlm.nih.gov/21834185.

xciii D. Cottrell, 'Engaging Young People in Treatment After Self-harm' (2013), https://adc.bmj.com/content/98/10/749.

xciv National Institute for Health and Clinical Excellence, 'Self-Harm'.

xcv For example, World Suicide and Self-harm Prevention Day, and organisations such as The Samaritans (www.samaritans.ie).

xcvi www.pieta.ie.

Index

Affordable Care Act, USA
(Obamacare), 175
Alcoholics Anonymous, 192
Antidepressants, 239, 241
Anxiety
tools to manage, 235–7
Attention deficit hyperactivity
disorder (ADHD), 158
AUDIT, 253–5
Autism, 158
Aware (organisation), 208

Balancing work, rest and play, 65
Balint, Michael, 128
Beck, Aaron T., 89, 90, 206, 230
Benzodiazepines, 256
Bipolar mood disorder, 157
Blake, William, 134
Breakdown, 139–40
Burnout, 96

Cannabis (see Marijuana)
Capra, Frank, 215
Caring for others, 179–83
CHIME – five features of
recovery, 4, 6, 146, 168,
181, 187, 201, 209,
216–22
Cognitive behavioural therapy
(CBT), 131, 205–6
Collaboration, 278–80
Comfort eating, 44
Compassion, 63, 98
Connectedness, 29, 216

Contemplation,
Precontemplation, 15,
16
Counselling, 125–30
COVID-19, 3, 41, 123, 169, 172,
184, 201, 208, 214, 223,
227

Dalai Lama, 66
Death, 101, 104
Decision Support Service, 106
Depression, 239, 242
Diary-keeping, 47, 228
Disclosure, 92
Distress, 188, 202–12
Drug misuse, 255

Eight dimensions of health, 4, 5
Emotional health, 30
Empowerment, 221
Environmental health, 26
Environment and mental health,
167
Equality legislation, 93–4
Erikson, Erik, 149
Exercise, 56

Financial health, 23
Five ways to wellness, 8–9, 176,
209, 226
Foucault, Michel, 214
Francis, Sir Robert, 269
Frankl, Viktor, 198, 219
'Fright, fight and flight', 121, 197

Gender and mental health, 157–60

Grief, 102–4

Grow (organisation), 208

HALT – hungry, angry, lonely and tired, 192, 201

Hanks, Tom, 265

Health Committee of the Medical Council, 271

Health, looking after, 84

Healthy eating plan, 37, 46

Heaney, Seamus, 243

Hearing Voices Network, 262

Hobbes, Thomas, 4

Hope, 184, 279–80

Identity, 142–53, 226

Infectious disease, 169, 189

Inflammation, 59

Institutional abuse, 160

Intellectual health, 27

It's a Wonderful Life, 212–15

Judgement, 71

Kindness, 222–4

Leaper, Dr Richard, 211

'Let there be nothing about me which is without me', 142, 219

Letting things go, 68

LGBTQ, 157

Life events (major and minor), 190–4

Lightening the load (see Balancing work, rest and play)

Light pollution, 167–8

Listening, 132, 242–6

Lynch, Thomas, 103

Major depressive disorder (clinical depression), 64

Marijuana, 258–60

Marmot, Michael, 23, 79, 97

Martin, Fr James, 207

Maslach, Christina, 96

Maslow's hierarchy of needs, 76–7

McVerry, Fr Peter, 178

Mediterranean diet, 43

Mental health ('facts'), 119
    difficulties (enduring), 119
    naming our difficulty, 134

Mid Staffordshire Hospital UK, 269

Mindfulness, 13, 37, 62, 236, 248
    practising a mindful attitude, 84

National Children's Hospital, 173–4

Negative automatic thoughts (NATs), 88–92, 131

New Economics Foundation (NEF), 8

Noctor, Colman, 82

Obsessive compulsive disorder (OCD), 157

Occupational health, 24

Panic anxiety, 246–8
Philbin Bowman, Abie, 165
Physical health, 21
Pieta House, 276
Porter, Michael, 177
Post-traumatic stress disorder
    (PTSD), 264–7
Practitioner health, 271
Psychosis, 260–4
    post-partum, 158
Psychotherapy (see Counselling)
Public health / Population health,
    169–79

Reassurance, 185
Recovery, 185, 194, 212, 216,
    232, 270
Reframing, 230–1
Relationship breakdown, 99
Resilience, 216, 233–5
Rogers, Carl, 199, 243
Routine and structure, 228

Samaritans, 133
Schizophrenia, 157
Self-harm, 272–6
Self-identification (see Identity)
Shipman, Harold, 270
Shultz, George, 260
Sleep, 5–6, 167
Social health, 28
Spiritual health, 31
Stewart, Jimmy, 213, 215
Stigma, 162
St Patrick's University Hospital,
    165, 210, 212
Stress, 188, 196–202

Substance Abuse and Mental
Health Services Administration
(SAMHSA-USA), 21
Suicide, 107–16
    talking to children
    about, 110
Sullenberger, Captain, 264–7
Swimming, 57

Tabula rasa, 129
Taking issues step by step, 83
'Technologies of the self', 214
Thatcher, Margaret, 50
THC, 258–60
'The Art of Collaboration', 278
Therapy (see Counselling)

Vaillant, George, 100
Value in healthcare, 177
Varadkar, Leo, 229
Vergangenheitsbewältigung, 162

Walk in My Shoes, 165
Wellness, 133
Who am I? 145–53
Will, living, 105
Work
    conflict at, 85–7
    discrimination at, 25, 94
    load, support and
    control at, 80
    stress at, 76
    synergy in the
    workplace, 80–1
    work–life balance, 82,
    271

Zoonosis, 41